WOMEN AND LEADERSHIP DEVELOPMENT IN COLLEGE

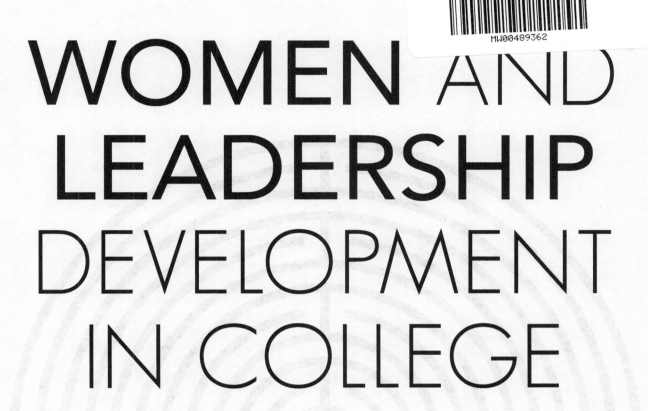

WOMEN AND
LEADERSHIP
DEVELOPMENT

WOMEN AND LEADERSHIP DEVELOPMENT IN COLLEGE

A Facilitation Resource

Jennifer M. Pigza, Julie E. Owen, and Associates

FOREWORD BY
Paige Haber-Curran and Daniel Tillapaugh

1996–2021 25TH ANNIVERSARY

Stylus
PUBLISHING, LLC.

STERLING, VIRGINIA

Sty/us

Published by Stylus Publishing, LLC.
22883 Quicksilver Drive
Sterling, Virginia 20166-2019

Library of Congress Cataloging-in-Publication Data
Names: Pigza, Jennifer M., editor. | Owen, Julie E., editor.
Title: Women and leadership development in college : a facilitation resource / [edited by] Jennifer M. Pigza, Julie E. Owen and associates ; foreword by Paige Haber-Curran and Daniel Tillapaugh.
Description: First edition. | Sterling, Virginia : Stylus Publishing, LLC., 2021. | Includes bibliographical references and index. | Summary: "This text is a detailed resource for anyone interested in women and leadership education, whether through a full-length course, a weekend workshop, or a one-time topical session. Each module includes includes learning objectives, detailed instructions, and ideas for adapting the module to diverse learning spaces and audiences"-- Provided by publisher.
Identifiers: LCCN 2021017927 (print) | LCCN 2021017928 (ebook) | ISBN 9781642670127 (cloth) | ISBN 9781642670134 (paperback) | ISBN 9781642670141 (adobe pdf) | ISBN 9781642670158 (epub)
Subjects: LCSH: Leadership in women. | Leadership--Study and teaching (Higher)
Classification: LCC HQ1150 .W645 2021 (print) | LCC HQ1150 (ebook) | DDC 303.3/4082--dc23
LC record available at https://lccn.loc.gov/2021017927
LC ebook record available at https://lccn.loc.gov/2021017928

Printed in the United States of America

All first editions printed on acid-free paper that meets the American National Standards Institute Z39-48 Standard.

Bulk Purchases

Quantity discounts are available for use in workshops and for staff development.

Call 1-800-232-0223

First Edition, 2021

To us all: May we become the leaders the world is waiting for.

Contents

SECTION EIGHT: REIMAGINING WOMEN AND LEADERSHIP: STRATEGIES, ALLIES, AND CRITICAL HOPE

Foreword

Paige Haber-Curran and Daniel Tillapaugh

Fifteen years ago we met in graduate school and immediately connected over our passion for student leadership development. Our interest in facilitating opportunities to develop leadership capacity in students stemmed from our own experiences as undergraduate students. Dan was a prominent student leader, serving as his campus's student body president and a resident assistant. Paige had extensive experience as a peer leader within a 4-year comprehensive leadership program and was intrigued by how to empower individuals who may not self-identify as leaders to engage in opportunities to develop their leadership capacity. During our graduate studies we gained ample experience in leadership education through developing, teaching, and facilitating curricular and cocurricular leadership experiences for undergraduate students. We also began our scholarly pursuits in the field, working alongside and learning from and with incredible leadership scholars and educators.

Fast-forward a few years, and we once again were studying and working together as doctoral students. Naturally, the topic of leadership development was central to many of our conversations. Our coursework challenged us to think about leadership and about ourselves in different ways, which in turn had an impact on the undergraduate leadership courses we taught. Many of our course dialogues focused on the role of identity in leadership—reflecting on our own experiences as learners and teachers, modeling this reflection for the students in our courses, and encouraging the same from the students.

One semester, Paige taught an undergraduate course on women's leadership. There were 12 exceptional women in the course, eager to explore leadership through the lens of gender and with a focus on their identity as women. As a group, they peeled back the layers of their respective identities, troubled the concept of leadership, and grew in their sense of self as women and as leaders. For one class session, Dan enjoyed guest lecturing, discussing the ways that gender is socialized and mediated by other forms of identity. The course and the space cocreated alongside the students was truly a gift.

We reminisce on these particular experiences in light of Jennifer Pigza, Julie Owen, and their associates' contributions in *Women and Leadership Development in College: A Facilitation Resource*. In the 10 years since Paige's instruction of the women's leadership course, there has been an incredible amount of work done to advance the topic of identity and leadership—particularly women and leadership.

In 2017, we coedited a monograph on critical perspectives on gender and student leadership in the *New Directions for Student Leadership* series. In that work, we wrote:

We encourage leadership educators to be bold and innovative in their work and to help students become critical consumers of what they are learning about leadership through a critical, gendered lens. . . . Our students are living in a world that requires new ways of thinking about identity, particularly gender, and leadership; our leadership programs should be a reflection of that world. (Haber-Curran & Tillapaugh, 2017, pp. 19–20)

Our hope, at the time of writing that, was that leadership scholars and educators would connect more to critical theory, particularly intersectionality, feminist theory, and critical race theory, to gain a more critical perspective on leadership to inform their leadership education practice. In *Women and Leadership Development in College: A Facilitation Guide*, Drs. Pigza and Owen have responded to that call by cultivating a network of collaborators actively committed to socially just feminist leadership. These editors and authors bring direct professional experience working to support women and their leadership on their campuses and in their communities. As the editors of this text, Drs. Pigza and Owen continue to model what it means to be women practicing strong, collaborative, and effective leadership built on the foundation of engaging in ethical, critical, relational practices. Their work here as well as in their professional roles straddles true liberatory praxis, by using theory in practice to effect change.

This book is a testament to their commitment to helping all students—but centering women, in particular—think critically about the ways gender and leadership are intertwined in systems of power, privilege, and oppression. The lessons provided in this text promise to serve as powerful learning experiences for learners to gain critical self-awareness around their own identities and leadership practice. This text is a gift to the field of leadership education and will undoubtedly empower and help prepare the next generation of leaders in our society.

References

Haber-Curran, P., & Tillapaugh, D. (2017). Gender and student leadership. In D. Tillapaugh & P. Haber-Curran (Eds.), *Critical perspectives on gender and student leadership* (New Directions for Student Leadership, No. 154; pp. 11–22). Jossey-Bass.

Biography

Paige Haber-Curran, PhD, is associate professor and program coordinator for the student affairs in higher education program at Texas State University.

Daniel Tillapaugh, PhD, is assistant professor and chair in the Department of Counselor Education at California Lutheran University.

Preface

Julie E. Owen

In her book *Teaching to Transgress: Education as the Practice of Freedom*, author bell hooks (1994) reminds us that "The classroom remains the most radical space of possibility in the academy" (p. 1). If you believe in the transformative power of education, it naturally follows to wonder how to create such radical spaces of possibility.

This may be a provocative statement, but I believe that who you are is how you teach. As educators, our own values/philosophies/disciplines/identities shape the curriculum and culture of our classes. In order to create inclusive spaces, we must continue to interrogate our own lenses and positions, and to the extent possible share that learning process with students. Why would students risk vulnerability, reflection, and challenge if we are unable to model it ourselves?

As we do our own work it becomes imperative to also invite students to explore their own personal and social identities and how these shape their learning. Educators should situate learning in students' experiences (especially vital for women and for students from underrepresented backgrounds), validate students as self-authored knowers, and help students understand the socially constructed nature of knowledge and its application. Paradoxically, the best teaching and learning is both individualized and collective. It is an educator's job to help students develop the habits of mind needed to effectively engage in personal, professional, and public life. This involves welcoming the whole student into the classroom, not just discrete parts of their being. We must intentionally teach students habits of integration. By this I mean to integrate their in and out of classroom experiences, to seek connections across diverse disciplines and sources of knowledge, and to feel comfortable functioning as both teacher and learner.

This facilitator's guide is a stand-alone resource that also serves as a companion to *We Are the Leaders We've Been Waiting For: Women and Leadership Development in College* (Owen, 2020). Jennifer Pigza and I worked with many talented collaborators to develop exercises designed to surface concepts of identity, intersectionality, integration, power, and critical perspectives in leadership. While designed to explicitly "teach" the core concepts covered in the *We Are the Leaders We've Been Waiting For* text, these activities can be adapted for use in formal or informal learning spaces, as part of the cocurriculum and curricula, and for the nature and purposes of participants. This *Facilitation Resource* presents 35 modules for ideas and themes covered in each chapter of the accompanying text. Each module includes the basics (like group size, time required, methods, and materials), learning objectives, and detailed instructions.

Several modules explicitly address the role of storytelling and autoethnography in leadership learning. One way to explore the important ideas about the social construction of feminism and leadership, and about the nature of critical thinking, reflection, and critical theory, is to invite students to consider how these ideas connect to their own gender and leadership journey. The use of narrative can be a profound tool for self-revelation, reflection, and healing. Stories are powerful because they allow others to access our thoughts, feelings, and experiences, and hopefully to find connections. They also allow us to make connections among experiences that we may not have realized before. Counternarratives, or telling and listening to stories from those who have been historically marginalized, create empowerment and agency to those who may previously have been silenced, and can create understanding and connection across listeners.

Here are but a few of the critical questions that are implicitly and explicitly addressed throughout the *Facilitation Resource.*

- How do we make explicit the complexities of power within education and prepare individuals and collectives to navigate it?
- How can we interrogate/deconstruct dominant narratives? Whose voices are missing/silenced in classroom content and processes?
- How do we understand intersectional identities (of ourselves and of our students)

in the classroom? To what extent are we engaged in examining our own assumptions, preferences, blind spots, identities?

- How do our own values/philosophies/identities shape the curriculum and culture of our programs/classes? What are implications for introducing critical perspectives in the classroom as they relate to intersecting identities?
- Do the social locations of those practicing education replicate dominant norms?

As leadership educators shift from teacher-centered to learner-centered environments, from hierarchical to shared responsibility for learning, and from absolute to constructed ways of knowing, these inclusive pedagogies model the kinds of authentic learning we want for those engaging in leadership.

References

hooks, b. (1994). *Teaching to transgress: Education as the practice of freedom.* Routledge.

Owen, J. E. (2020). *We are the leaders we've been waiting for: Women and leadership development in college.* Stylus.

Acknowledgments

Our gratitude begins with students—past, present, and future—who are at the heart of why we engage in education as a practice of equity and justice. We practice, we fail, we learn, we practice some more. Our students elicit the best in us, call us out, and draw us in. Thank you for your invocation that we continue to learn.

We are grateful for the community of leadership educators and practitioners you encounter in these pages. Without them, this book would not be the diverse collection of voices, wisdom, and practice that you see. Without them, we—Jennifer and Julie—would not be as enriched and emboldened as we are as educators and humans. Thank you for saying YES.

This idea came to fruition because of the confidence and patience of John von Knorring, the detailed and persistent eyes of Alexandra Hartnett, and the entire team at Stylus Publishing. We appreciate your support and guidance throughout this process.

From Jennifer

In this moment of gratitude, I am reminded of three phrases about being and becoming.

First, from education philosopher Maxine Greene: "I am . . . not yet." I am grateful to those who see in me what I often cannot yet see in myself. Among them are Rachel Bauman, Susan R. Komives, Janet Luce, Robert Nash, and Julie Owen. Thank you.

Second, is the Zulu phrase, *ubuntu*, meaning "I am, because you are." Thank you to my friends and colleagues at Saint Mary's College of California. I am especially grateful to Shawny Anderson for supporting my request for dedicated time to work on this book and to my colleagues in the Catholic Institute for Lasallian Social Action for creating with me a culture of leadership based in equity, authenticity, and risk-taking.

Finally, a quote from my wife, Frances Sweeney, who invites us every day to "Just Love," meaning that love is our singular purpose in life and that love is what makes justice possible. She loves my not-yet-ness, and thank you is never enough.

From Julie

While my name is listed as a coeditor of this volume, it is far and away predominantly a product of the hard work and coordinating efforts of my wise and witty colleague and friend, Jennifer Pigza. To her go all accolades and praise. This volume had its nexus during a weekend getaway we had in Tahoe—JP, I cannot wait to see what emerges from our next trip! I couldn't ask for a better companion on this journey.

I second Jennifer's gratitude for the brilliant and patient contributors who lent their time and talents to producing such thought-provoking and engaging learning modules. I have had the great joy of pilot-testing many of these modules in my classes. On behalf of all the learners who have and will experience your pedagogical gifts and critical questions, we are profoundly grateful.

Appreciation to my family—Connie, Ken, Laura, and Bennett—and to my fur family, Max and Mini, who kept me company on this journey. Extra special thanks to Susan R. Komives—the most generous and generative leadership educator whose shoulders we all stand on—none of this would exist if not for you. I treasure your lifelong mentorship and friendship—tiaras forever!

How to Use This Resource

Women and Leadership Development in College: A Facilitation Resource is both a chapter-by-chapter companion to *We Are the Leaders We've Been Waiting For: Women and Leadership Development in College* (Owen, 2020) as well as a stand-alone resource that can be used in a variety of higher education and community settings.

This text is also a community effort. As you dive into these modules, you join a collective of nearly 30 leadership educators who are in conversation about how to facilitate the leadership learning and development of college students. We welcome you to the conversation. Whether you are exploring and experimenting as a leadership educator, seeking validation for your good instincts, or feeling confirmed in your identity as a leadership educator, you are welcome in these pages. We hope these modules both inspire your own teaching and facilitation and maximize your preparation time.

The presumed audiences for most of the modules are undergraduate and graduate students who are engaged in a leadership development activity or program focused on women and/or gender. You will notice, however, that the modules can be used (or adapted for use) with fellow faculty and staff, high school students, faith communities, and community members in nonprofit, public, private, and for-profit sectors. We encourage your creative adaptation of these

modules in as many settings and groups as possible. Here's where you might utilize this resource:

- Credit-bearing leadership classes
- Stand-alone workshops or training
- Multiday retreats
- Community-based workshops or training
- Group development

To make it easy for you to use, sections of this book are organized around the chapters of the companion text. Each section begins with a brief summary, and each module is a stand-alone lesson plan that includes all the details and instructions you will need to translate theory into practice. While presented as in-person experiences, most of these modules can be translated into synchronous or asynchronous online environments. The module details include:

- Setup
- Overview
- Learning outcomes
- Step-by-step directions
- Facilitator notes
- References

As you dive into the *Facilitation Resource*, you will notice that the modules' activities have varying times and levels of complexity. You will also notice a mixture of hands-on, conversational, theory-based, and practice-based approaches. Echoing the practice in Owen (2020), many modules include storytelling and narrative as a pathway to leadership development. This variety is intentional so that facilitators can choose the modules that best fit your context, such as who your participants are, how much time you have, and how experienced you are as a teacher and facilitator. You can adapt the modules to fit your situation, and often, resources like this serve as a springboard for our own creativity and particular application needs.

Ultimately, the contributors to this facilitator's guide invite you to make this work your own. Follow the modules as presented, modify them to fit your situation, riff off them to create your own plans, combine elements of several in a mash-up module. Accompanying students in their leadership learning and development is an honor and a joy, and joining efforts with you in these pages expands our shared practice and pedagogy of hope.

Reference

Owen, J. E. (2020). *We are the leaders we've been waiting for: Women and leadership development in college.* Stylus.

SECTION ONE

A Critical Moment for Women and Leadership

The modules in this section dive into the social and historical contexts for women and leadership as well as the evolution of leadership theory. This includes a review of the three waves of feminism and the suggestion of the emergence of a fourth wave founded on intersectional approaches and global consciousness. The effects of systems of privilege and oppression on how people experience both feminism and leadership are explored. This section also includes a foundation module on the terminology of gender.

Key Ideas

- Hegemony and ideology
- Waves of feminism
- Gender identity
- Evolution of leadership theory
- Intersectionality

Dominant Ideologies and Hegemonic Mechanisms Impacting Women's Leadership

R.J. Youngblood

- Group size: Any size group. For larger groups, consider dividing participants into groups of 3–4 to facilitate more meaningful discussion and engagement.
- Time: 60 minutes
- Methods used: video, small group discussion, critical methods of analysis
- Materials needed: Video clip from *They Live* (Carpenter, 1988). The clip can be found on YouTube as "They Live Sunglasses" (Stoolie33, 2012); and additional artifacts as described in the Facilitator Notes.

Overview

This activity invites participants to develop a deeper understanding of how dominant ideologies and hegemonic mechanisms might influence, subjugate, or delegitimize the leadership of women. Participants will be asked to reflect on their assumptions and lenses that they use to make sense of systems and make connections to how they understand women's leadership.

Learning Outcomes

- Identify dominant ideologies and hegemonic mechanisms
- Analyze hegemony and ideology in the context of leadership

Directions

1. *Preparation.* Review the video clip and facilitation questions. Identify and print artifacts for small groups to analyze.
2. *Introduction* (5 minutes). As a large group, review the ideas of ideology, hegemony, and the social construction of knowledge. Ask participants for their input about how they would define each of the terms. A reference point for these meanings is Owen (2020).
   a. Ideology: "The broadly accepted values, beliefs, myths, and explanations that appear to be true and desirable to a majority of the population" (p. 193).
   b. Hegemony: "A form of social control whereby dominated or subordinate classes of people consent to their own domination" (p. 193).

c. Social construction of knowledge: "Refers to the process by which society and culture interact to create a host of meanings and associations about what is meant by certain words" (p. 199).

3. *Video and Response* (10–15 minutes). As a large group, spend 3–4 minutes viewing the video clip from *They Live* (Carpenter, 1988). Facilitate a large group discussion for 5–10 minutes to help participants debrief the *They Live* clip and to develop a deeper understanding of the concepts of ideology and hegemony. Ask for general responses to the video and pose these questions:

   a. What gives the character the ability to see ideology in the clip?
   b. What gives someone interested in exercising leadership the ability to see ideology?
   c. Where do you see ideology at play in your everyday interactions?
   d. What hidden messages have you learned about leadership—consciously or unconsciously?

4. *Small Groups* (10–15 minutes). Divide participants into groups of 3–4 people and provide each group an artifact (described in the Facilitator Notes). Using the following questions, direct small groups to engage in conversation. Participants will respond to questions that guide them to analyze their artifact and identify dominant ideologies and hegemonic mechanisms. Questions:

   a. Who is the audience of this message?
   b. What is a likely intended conscious message?
   c. What is a likely unconscious message?
   d. Who benefits from the dominant message?
   e. Who is disadvantaged as a result of the dominant message?
   f. What are the implications of not acknowledging the unconscious messages included in your artifact?
   g. How do people resist the relationship communicated in these messages?

5. *Large Group Discussion* (5–10 minutes). Ask the small groups to reconvene and have each small group share something from their discussion. Debrief the artifact analysis experience with the large group and connect the learning to women and leadership.

   a. When are hegemonic mechanisms at play when women are attempting to enact leadership? Provide an example.
   b. How do you see your identity at work within a system?

6. *Debrief* (10 minutes). Take the pulse of the group. For some, this might have been a challenging conversation. Remind participants that this is just the beginning of conversations that help them be more aware of their worldviews. As facilitator, supporting the group to co-emerge meaning from shared dialogue is essential to develop the learning community's leadership capacity. Return to the small group questions for large-group debriefing. Also ask further questions that engage curiosity and openness and explore a similar line of inquiry reflected in the module.

   a. How do identity, power, and systems show up (or not) in our analysis?
   b. What are we not discussing here? What voices and perspectives are missing?
   c. How might we interrogate our assumptions and complicate what seems clear?

Facilitator Notes

This activity is most successful when facilitated with current events or examples to help bridge thinking from abstract concepts to how participants might identify dominant ideologies and hegemony as it relates to the issues of women and leadership in their own contexts. Artifact examples are images, advertisements, social media exchanges, articles, current events, or artifacts that identify and point to examples of ideology in action. Artifacts can be tailored to be developmentally appropriate and resonate with the context of the group. Search the internet for examples such as these:

- professional and unprofessional women's hairstyles
- the Claire McCaskill and Alexandria Ocasio-Cortez "shiny object" exchange
- female comic book characters (see The Hawkeye Initiative and critiques)
- fashion advertisements
- women breastfeeding in public
- Serena Williams's catsuit
- women in the infantry

References	Biography

Carpenter, J. (Director). (1988). *They live* [Film]. Universal Pictures.

Owen, J. E. (2020). *We are the leaders we've been waiting for: Women and leadership development in college.* Stylus.

Stoolie33. (2012, August 1). *They live sunglasses* [Video file]. https://www.youtube.com/watch?v=JI8AMRbqY6w

R. J. Youngblood is the assistant director of the Academic Achievement Center and a doctoral student in the Leadership Communication program at Kansas State University.

Understanding the Terminology of Gender

Daniel Tillapaugh

- Group size: Open to any size group, although if you have a large group of over 20 participants, you may want to divide up into smaller groups
- Time: 45 minutes to 1 hour
- Methods: Individual reflection, small group discussion, video component
- Materials needed: Video and projector equipment, newsprint, markers, sticky notes, copies of Gender Unicorn handout (Pan & Moore, n.d.)—a copy for each participant
- Multimedia: There are a multitude of very helpful and educational short videos available online which explore discussions and definitions of gender and sex. For a two and a half minute video that is a good primer on terminology of gender, see NowThis World (2015).

Overview

The messages individuals learn about leadership throughout their lives are often deeply connected to the socialization of gender roles and expectations (Tillapaugh & Haber-Curran, 2017). However, leadership development and education often does not adequately address those connections (Haber-Curran & Tillapaugh, 2018). In this module, facilitators are equipped with ideas to help participants understand the terminology of gender and why understanding these concepts are essential for one's leadership practice.

Learning Outcomes

- Understand concepts of gender and their application to leadership
- Critically reflect upon the ways that the socialization of gender has affected participants' lives and their views of leadership

Directions

1. *Preparation.* On one piece of newsprint, write "Earliest memory of becoming aware of your gender." On another piece of newsprint, write "Earliest memory of becoming aware of gender norms and expectations." Place these two pieces of newsprint on the walls.
2. *Introduction* (5 minutes). Before starting this activity, the facilitator should begin by saying that individuals will be asked to engage in

some reflective discussions during this module. Some of the exercises will ask them to talk about their own lives and their experiences, so if the group has shared community agreements or expectations, it would be helpful to review those. If not, the facilitator should ask that what is shared in the group should not be shared outside of the group and that stories and insights individuals share should not be shared with others outside of the group. Individuals should be affirmed that they can participate to the level at which they are most comfortable.

3. *Personal Reflection* (8 minutes). Provide a couple of small sticky notes to each participant. Ask them to spend a few minutes reflecting on their earliest memory of when they became aware of their gender growing up and also their earliest memory through a personal example of specific gender norms and expectations. The facilitator may want to give a personal example from their own lived experiences for both to help the participants jumpstart their thinking. Ask the participants to write their examples of each on the sticky notes provided. After 5 minutes of reflection time, ask participants to place their written example on their sticky note up on the newsprint that corresponds to their answer.

4. *Small Groups* (10 minutes). Divide the groups into two groups and assign each to one of the newsprints. Instruct the participants to review the sticky notes and note any patterns or themes that emerge from the examples provided. Ask each group to take notes and select a spokesperson to report out to the large group. Give the groups approximately 8 minutes to complete this step.

5. *Large Group Conversation* (10 minutes). Have the groups report out any themes or patterns that they found within their discussions. Provide ample time to debrief these conversations as a large group. For instance, the facilitator may ask:

a. Was there a general age at which individuals are first becoming aware of their gender?

b. For some individuals, their example is something that they can still recall that happened decades ago; what stands out to you about that? Why do you think this may still be present for them?

c. In what ways can gender roles and expectations be helpful? How can they be harmful?

d. Think about the messages you have gotten about gender throughout your life; how have these messages been internalized?

6. *Video and Debrief* (7 minutes). From there, the facilitator should segue into a discussion of how important it is to engage in a critical understanding of gender to be able to effectively understand aspects of one's leadership practice. To begin this process, the group will watch a short video clip that provides some information about terminology around gender. Play the chosen video for the participants. After the video ends, invite individuals to reflect about the terminology that was covered in the clip. Ask if anyone learned anything new from the clip and, if so, what might have been new information. Invite any questions or clarify any confusion students might have from the video.

7. *Gender Unicorn Handout* (10 minutes). Pass out the handout of The Gender Unicorn to each participant. Highlight and redefine the various aspects of The Gender Unicorn, including the gender identity, gender expression, sex assigned at birth, and physical and emotional attraction constructs. Point out how each of these constructs is represented by an icon that is placed on the unicorn itself to show how gender identity is a self-construct while gender expression is an external manifestation of the unicorn's gender through apparel and appearance and so forth. Ask the participants to fill in their own gender and sex identity by placing a dot or an x on each spectra (for more information see Pan & Moore, n.d.).

8. *Closing Conversation* (10 minutes). Engage the group in a debriefing conversation about why it is important to think about this

terminology of gender as it relates to the larger concept of leadership. The facilitator might ask some of the following questions:

a. As you think about what we have covered today, what is important about being aware of terminology around gender? In what ways does this matter as it relates to leadership?

b. Think about young children. Why is it that young boys who are assertive are recognized as leaders whereas young girls who are assertive are more likely to be labeled bossy?

c. As The Gender Unicorn reminds us, there is a false binary of gender being a man and a woman that gets reinforced over and over within our society. How does this false binary get replicated within our daily lives? What examples can you think of in which we reinforce this binary? How is this problematic?

d. Based upon what you've learned today, what is one takeaway that you have from this conversation?

Facilitator Notes

Facilitators of this module need to have a good grasp on the distinctions between sex and gender. They should not feel as though they have to know everything about these concepts, but engaging in some advance preparation by reading about gender or dialoguing with colleagues may be a helpful start. Modeling the fact that much of our understanding about gender is ever-changing and evolving, and that it's important to stay connected to that larger discourse, will be a helpful framing for the participants.

Prior to having the participants complete The Gender Unicorn activity and place a dot or x to signify their own gender identity, the facilitator may want to

complete the task and then walk participants through the activity by sharing his/her/hir/zir/their own gender identity. This can also provide helpful modeling of critically reflecting on one's gender identity for students who may not have thought much about their gender before.

Additionally, it is strongly encouraged that facilitators of this activity might think about gender-based resources that are available on campus or in the local community. Pulling together a list of these resources (i.e., gender studies majors or minors on campus, LGBTQ+ resource centers, youth groups around gender) may be helpful to distribute at the end of the session so that individuals who are interested in exploring more around this topic might have a good first step in doing so.

References

Haber-Curran, P., & Tillapaugh, D. (2018). Beyond the binary: Advancing socially just leadership through the lens of gender. In K. L. Guthrie & V. S. Chunoo (Eds.), *Changing the narrative: Socially just leadership education* (pp. 77–92). Information Age.

NowThis World. (July 27, 2015). *Sex & gender identity: An intro* [Video]. YouTube. https://www.youtube.com/watch?v=ago78PhUofI

Pan, L., & Moore, A. (n.d.). *The gender uniorn.* Trans Student Educational Resources. http://www.transstudent.org/gender/

Tillapaugh, D., & Haber-Curran, P. (2017). Gender and student leadership: A critical examination. In D. Tillapaugh & P. Haber-Curran (Eds.), *Critical perspectives on gender and student leadership* (New Directions for Student Leadership, No. 154, pp. 11–22). Jossey-Bass.

Biography

Daniel Tillapaugh, PhD, is assistant professor and chair in the Department of Counselor Education at California Lutheran University.

Reviewing the Three (Four?) Waves of Feminism

Heather D. Shea

- Group size: any size (but probably works best with fewer than 25)
- Time: 45–60 minutes
- Methods: interactive "move about the room" activity
- Materials: Historical event cards, "wave" year cards, tape, and sticky notes.

Overview

In this interactive timeline activity, participants will review and reflect on the historical and social contexts in which women and leadership is situated, with specific attention to the U.S. "waves" of feminism. This activity is designed to be interactive and engaging with group discussion.

Learning Outcomes

- Name the three (four?) waves of feminism in the United States
- Identify significant symbolic, historical, and cultural events that occurred during each wave
- Examine how feminism's evolution relates to the advancement of women in leadership roles during each era

Directions

1. *Preparation.*
   a. Write out the following dates on index cards and distribute them across the wall of the room: Before 1850, 1850s, 1860s, 1870s, 1880s, 1890s, 1900s, 1910s, 1920s, 1930s, 1940s, 1950s, 1960s, 1970s, 1980s, 1990s, 2000s, 2010s–present, UNKNOWN.
   b. Prepare a summary handout for each wave of feminism; you should have four waves (four worksheets) for small group work. The worksheet should include: dates of "wave," major accomplishments, disappointments, significant leaders, significant tactics, and what makes this a "wave" of feminism?
   c. Copy one set of the Feminist Wave Cards (at the back of this module). Variation: You could remove the "guessing" part of the activity but instead print cards in different colors based on the "wave."
2. *Introduction and Activity with Cards and Timeline* (5–10 minutes).
   a. The group leader moves about the room and distributes the Feminist Wave Cards evenly among the participants.

b. Individuals, using only their preexisting knowledge (no cheating by searching on phones!), estimate when the sociohistorical, cultural, or symbolic event on their card occurred and then tape that card on the timeline.

c. If the person doesn't have any idea where to put a card, they put it under the UNKNOWN category.

3. *Gallery Walk* (5–10 minutes). After all the cards have been placed on the timeline (or unknown area), distribute a few sticky notes to each participant. Invite participants to engage in a gallery walk, reading the cards and observing the locations; they should use the Post-it notes to make suggestions or comments (e.g., "this card belongs in the 1950s").

4. *Group Timeline Work* (10–15 minutes). Divide the group into five small groups. Each small group is responsible for a segment of the timeline (if desired, the group leader can give out the summary handout for each wave): Wave 1: pre-1840s to 1920s; Wave 2: 1960s to 1980s; Wave 3: 1990s to 2000s; Wave 4: 2000s to present; Unknown.

a. Each group looks at the cards adhered to the timeline during their era. At this point, they should make adjustments to the order (can use internet search, or look at the timeline key at the end of the lesson). The group should deliver misplaced cards to other groups as needed. Meanwhile, the "unknown" group (if there are no "unknown" cards, this isn't needed) will learn about the events that were put into "unknown" and accurately place them on the timeline.

b. Once the timeline and associated events are agreed upon, the small group looks collectively at the cards during their wave and answers the following questions:

i. Given the sociohistorical events that occurred during this timeframe, what was the overall goal (or goals) of the movement during this wave of feminism? What were the major accomplishments?

ii. Discuss in your group: What (in your opinion) was the most hopeful outcome

of the era? What was the most disappointing outcome (or missing outcome)?

iii. Who were the significant people during this era (either in the timeline or otherwise)? What kinds of messages/tactics did the feminist leaders in this wave use to push forth their initiatives during this era?

iv. What makes the era a "wave"?

v. What remains to be accomplished, what are the obstacles, and what role might feminist leadership play in overcoming them?

5. *Small Group Report Out* (10 minutes). Having taken some notes on their sign, the group should identify a few comments from their discussion to share out with the larger group. After reporting out, rearrange the room to facilitate a group debrief.

6. *Debriefing* (10 minutes). After concluding group reports, it might be helpful to debrief the activity. Here are a few prompts for group discussion:

a. Who decides when waves come and go?

b. Given your knowledge of history, what is missing? Whose history is left out?

c. Was this activity difficult or easy? Why do you think that was?

d. If you didn't use internet search, how accurate were you in your first estimation?

e. Are you surprised about what has (or has not) been accomplished throughout this timeline?

f. What role do women as leaders (and feminist leaders of any gender) play in this timeline? Who promoted these events?

Facilitator Notes

This is definitely an activity that will test students' recall of historical facts and timelines! It would be fine to utilize internet searches with available technology if the facilitator wants to speed up the process, however, the point can also be made that women's history is largely *not* taught, celebrated, or remembered. Therefore, if the "unknown" group has a large task (if many people don't know what era their card belongs to), this might be an interesting point to make. Please emphasize that this is not a personal/individual failing for which individuals should feel guilty, but rather the failing of our larger educational system. However, now that they're aware of the history they did not learn, perhaps the time is now.

Biography

Heather D. Shea, PhD, director of Women's Student Services and program lead for the Learning, Culture, Technology in Europe (LCTE) Education Abroad Program at Michigan State University.

Timeline Key for Handout 1.3.1

1791	Mary Wollstonecraft's book *A Vindication of the Rights of Woman* published
1848	Declaration of Sentiments published
1848	Seneca Falls Convention held in Seneca Falls, New York
1850	National Women's Rights Convention held in Worchester, Massachusetts
1851	Sojourner Truth gives her speech, "Ain't I a Woman?"
1855	University of Iowa becomes the first coeducational public or state university in the United States
1870	Louisa Swain became the first woman to vote in a general election, in Laramie, Wyoming
1916	Margaret Sanger, birth control activist, established the first birth control clinic in the United States.
1920	19th Amendment ratified (women's right to vote)
1929	Virginia Woolf's *A Room of One's Own* is published
1938	The Fair Labor Standards Act establishes minimum wage without regard to sex
1949	Simone de Beauvoir's *The Second Sex* is published
1963	Betty Friedan publishes *The Feminine Mystique*
1963	Equal Pay Act passed (theoretically outlawed the gender pay gap)
1964	Sexual harassment legislation in the workplace
1964	Title VII of the Civil Rights Act passes including a prohibition against employment discrimination on the basis of race, color, religion, national origin, or sex
1968	Miss America Pageant protests staged by the Redstockings, the New York Radical Feminists, and others
1968	No mass burning of bras in protest occurred, but women gathered to protest women's objectification by discarding bras and copies of *Playboy*
1968	The BITCH Manifesto is published
1970	Title IX
1970	Shulamith Firestone publishes *The Dialectic of Sex: The Case for Feminist Revolution*
1970s	"The Personal Is Political" expression is popularized
1972	First edition of *Ms.* magazine published
1972	Women are allowed to run the Boston Marathon
1972	The ERA passed the Senate and was sent to the states for ratification
1973	Roe v. Wade guarantees women reproductive freedom
1974	Women receive the right to hold credit cards and apply for mortgages (in their own names)
1978	Pregnancy Discrimination Act enacted
1982	The deadline for the ratification of the Equal Rights Amendment passed, without the ERA being ratified
1983	Alice Walker writes, "Womanist Is to Feminist as Purple Is to Lavender"
1984	Audre Lorde publishes *Sister Outsider*
1987	Congress designates March as Women's History Month
1989	Kimberlé Crenshaw coined the term *intersectionality*
1990	Patricia Hill Collins publishes *Black Feminist Thought: Knowledge, Consciousness, and the Politics of Empowerment*
1990	Judith Butler publishes *Gender Trouble*, arguing that sex and gender are different
1990s	Riot grrl groups emerge in the music scene
1991	Anita Hill testifies before the Senate Judiciary Committee that nominee to the Supreme Court, Clarence Thomas, sexually harassed her at work

1992	The "Year of the Woman" was declared after 24 women won seats in the House of Representatives and three more won seats in the Senate	**2013**	Wendy Davis filibustered a Texas abortion law
1992	March for Women's Lives sponsored by NOW (National Organization for Women)	**2014**	Chimamanda Ngozi Adichie publishes *We Should All Be Feminists*
1993	Marital rape is outlawed	**2014**	Roxane Gay publishes *Bad Feminist*
1993	The Family and Medical Leave Act goes into effect	**2014–2015**	Rape survivor Emma Sulkowicz carries her mattress around Columbia University's campus waiting for the university to expel her rapist
1993	Joycelyn Elders became the first African American and first woman U.S. Surgeon General	**2015**	Sex discrimination outlawed in health insurance
2000	bell hooks publishes *Feminism Is for Everybody: Passionate Politics*	**2016**	#MeToo and #TimesUp explode in social media
2002	Rebecca Walker publishes an article in *Ms.* magazine in which she says "I am not a post-feminism feminist. I am the third-wave"	**2016**	Harvey Weinstein, and many other men in the entertainment industry, are accused of sexual misconduct, sexual harassment, and sexual assault
2008	Feminist blogs like *Jezebel* and *Feministing* spread across the internet	**2017, 2018 . . .**	Women's Marches across the globe
2009	The Lilly Ledbetter Fair Pay Act is signed into federal law	**2020**	Senator Kamala Harris, the daughter of Jamaican and Indian immigrants, becomes vice-president-elect of the United States

Handout 1.3.1 Waves of Feminism

Congress designates March as Women's History Month

The BITCH Manifesto is published

The deadline for the ratification of the Equal Rights Amendment passes without the ERA being ratified

Women receive the right to hold credit cards and apply for mortgages (in their own names)

Marital rape is outlawed

Sexual harassment legislation in the workplace

No mass burning of bras in protest occurred, but women gathered to protest women's objectification by discarding bras and copies of *Playboy*

First edition of *Ms.* magazine published

Anita Hill testifies before the Senate Judiciary Committee that nominee to the Supreme Court, Clarence Thomas, sexually harassed her at work

Harvey Weinstein, and many other prominent men in the entertainment industry, accused of sexual misconduct

The "Year of the Woman" declared after 24 women won seats in the House of Representatives and three more won seats in the Senate

March for Women's Lives sponsored by NOW (National Organization for Women)

Sex discrimination outlawed in health insurance

Roe v. Wade: The U.S. Supreme Court declares that the Constitution protects women's right to terminate an early pregnancy, thus making abortion legal in the United States

#MeToo and #TimesUp explode on social media

Women's Marches take place across the globe

Equal Pay Act passed (theoretically outlawed the gender pay gap)

Title IX of the Education Amendments prohibits sex discrimination in all aspects of education programs that receive federal support

Kimberlé Crenshaw coins the term *intersectionality*

Judith Butler publishes *Gender Trouble*, arguing that sex and gender are different

Rebecca Walker publishes an article in *Ms.* magazine in which she says "I am not a post-feminism feminist. I am the third-wave"

A rape survivor, Emma Sulkowicz, carries her mattress around Columbia University's campus, waiting for the university to expel her rapist

Wendy Davis filibusters a Texas abortion law

Pregnancy Discrimination Act enacted

Mary Wollstonecraft's book *A Vindication of the Rights of Woman* published

Seneca Falls Convention held in Seneca Falls, New York

Declaration of Sentiments published

National Women's Rights Convention held in Worchester, Massachusetts

Sojourner Truth gives her speech, "Ain't I a Woman?"

Louisa Swain became the first woman to vote in a general election, in Laramie, Wyoming

19th Amendment ratified (women's suffrage)

Margaret Sanger, birth control activist, establishes the first birth control clinic in the United States

Virginia Woolf's *A Room of One's Own* is published

Simone de Beauvoir's *The Second Sex* is published

University of Iowa becomes the first coeducational public or state university in the United States

Miss America Pageant protests staged by the Redstockings, the New York Radical Feminists, and others

"The Personal Is Political" expression is popularized

Shulamith Firestone publishes *The Dialectic of Sex: The Case for Feminist Revolution*

Audre Lorde publishes *Sister Outsider*

Betty Friedan publishes *The Feminine Mystique*

Patricia Hill Collins publishes *Black Feminist Thought: Knowledge, Consciousness, and the Politics of Empowerment*

The Lilly Ledbetter Fair Pay Act is signed into federal law

The Fair Labor Standards Act establishes minimum wage without regard to sex

Title VII of the Civil Rights Act passes including a prohibition against employment discrimination on the basis of race, color, religion, national origin, or sex

The Family and Medical Leave Act goes into effect

The ERA passes the Senate and is sent to the states for ratification

Joycelyn Elders becomes the first African American and first woman U.S. Surgeon General

Alice Walker writes, "Womanist Is to Feminist as Purple Is to Lavender"

Riot grrl groups emerge in the music scene and reclaim the word "girl." Bikini Kill lead singer writes, "BECAUSE we are angry at society that tells us Girl=Dumb, Girl=Bad, Girl=Weak"

bell hooks publishes *Feminism Is for Everybody: Passionate Politics*

Feminist blogs like *Jezebel* and *Feministing* spread across the internet

Chimamanda Ngozi Adichie publishes *We Should All Be Feminists*

Roxane Gay publishes *Bad Feminist*

"Add Women, Change Everything": Disrupting the Leadership Story Most Often Told

Natasha T. Turman and Shamika KariKari

- Group size: 4–20 participants
- Time: 90 minutes for Activity One, 25 minutes for Activity Two, 40 minutes for Activity Three
- Methods used: individual reflection, small and large group conversation
- Materials needed: paper, writing utensils, note cards, copies of charts described in each activity; this module draws heavily from Dugan (2017)
- Multimedia (optional): project the images of the charts and graphs for easier discussion

---

Overview

From a Western perspective, leadership—theory, practice, and development—has historically been understood and discussed through dominant leadership lenses. These dominant leadership lenses inadequately capture the leadership practice of a diverse republic. Ely et al. (2011) suggested that, "how people become leaders and how they take up the leader role are fundamentally questions about identity" (p. 476). Surprisingly, however, women, with their multiplicity of identities, are judged by leadership theories and held to standards of leadership practice that neglect consideration for diversity, identity, power, and context.

In order to attend to this, Dugan (2017) offered an approach to understanding and applying leadership theory that deconstructs the leadership story most often told and rebuilds it in more dynamic, culturally relevant, contextually bound, inclusive, and affirming ways. Dugan (2017) introduced the application of critical perspectives to leadership theory by utilizing interpretive tools of deconstruction and reconstruction to "call into question the nature of what we define as 'normal' as well as how the world and social relations operate" (p. 42).

Learning Outcomes

- Learn the tenets of deconstruction and reconstruction to assist in their interrogation of leadership theory
- Critique the leadership "story most often told" by critically examining their personal narratives to disrupt normativity
- Apply a critical lens to leadership theory to interrogate its implications for women

Directions

This module contains three activities that invite participants to deepen their knowledge of leadership theory from a critical perspective and to disrupt normative assumptions about leadership theory that position women as an exception and not the rule. The activities can be used across multiple gatherings or in one long workshop.

Activity One: Disrupting Your Leadership Norms (90 minutes)

Participants will learn the key tenets of deconstruction and reconstruction as identified by Dugan (2017) and begin to evaluate their own conceptualizations of leadership through those lenses.

1. *Preparation.* Provide participants with copies of the tools of deconstruction and reconstruction (Dugan, 2017, pp. 44 and 47).
2. *Introduction & Reading* (5 minutes). Distribute the handout and invite participants to read the handouts.
3. *Presentation* (20 minutes). As the facilitator, review each element of the handout.
4. *Pairs or Trios Deconstruction* (15 minutes). After review, have participants form pairs or trios. You may need to provide an example for participants using one of the tools of deconstruction and your own ideas. Also, it may be helpful to display the assignment prompts on a projector for the entire group as reference during the activity. Instruct students to:
   a. Brainstorm one leadership theory (e.g., relational leadership theory), leadership practice (e.g., engages in collective leadership), and/or leadership behavior/trait (e.g., nurturing) unique to women or socially attributed to women's leadership.
   b. Write down your ideas.
   c. Select at least one tool of deconstruction (e.g., willful blindness) and apply the tenets of that tool to critique the theory, practice, and/or behavior.
   d. Identify one critique and one rationale for your selection(s).
   e. Be prepared to discuss with a larger group.
5. *Large Group Discussion* (20 minutes)
   a. What inspired the leadership theory, practice, or behavior you identified?
   b. Why did you select the tool of deconstruction to interrogate this leadership domain?

   c. What critiques emerged as you attempted to apply this tool to understand women and leadership?
   d. What surprised you about yourself as you reflected on these findings?
6. *Pairs or Trios Reconstruction* (15 minutes). Have small groups reconvene to "reconstruct" their identified leadership theory, practice, or behavior. Instruct participants to:
   a. Revisit the identified leadership domains you just "deconstructed."
   b. Select at least one tool of reconstruction (e.g., disrupting normativity) and apply the tenets of that tool to reframe your identified leadership domain from a place that truly centers women and affirms and empowers.
7. *Large Group Synthesis and Conclusions* (15 minutes).
   a. What elements comprised your reconstruction?
   b. In what ways did you alter, adapt, or challenge your selected leadership theory, practice, or behavior using the "tools of reconstruction"?
   c. What factors did you consider to assess the best approach for reconstruction?

Activity 2: Typologies of Leadership: The Stories Most Often Told (25 minutes)

This activity focuses on comparing common conceptions of leadership typology to a critical typology of leadership. Grounded in a visual that describes the evolution of formal leadership theory, participants will identify key historical and/or personal events that reflect women and leadership to demonstrate how the "leadership story most often told" perpetuates dominant perspectives and places on the periphery women and communities of color (COC) who have been doing this "leadership" process and effecting change before there was a name for it.

1. *Preparation.* Make copies of a timeline that shows the evolution of leadership theory from the earliest forms within the industrial paradigm through the present forms within the post-industrial paradigm. Figure 3.1 from Dugan (2017) is one such image. An internet

search will provide several options useful for this activity.

2. *Introduction* (5 minutes). Provide participants with a copy of the evolution of formal leadership theory. Have participants look at the timeline and ask them to take 3–5 minutes and identify historical or personal events related to women and leadership. Be prepared to offer examples.

3. *Group Conversation* (5 minutes). Once participants have completed the self-reflection, ask for students to share events. As participants share, write those events on the timeline (have it projected or drawn on the whiteboard).

4. *Observation and Discussion* (10 minutes). Once you've hit a saturation point with contributions, ask students to offer their observations and offer some of your own observations about the events. Point out if there are key events missing or ask why they might have included certain events. Possible discussion questions:

   a. What is significant about the historical or personal event you selected?

   b. How has this event influenced/shaped your understanding of women and leadership? What about society's understanding?

   c. What stories are most often told about leadership? Do you see yourself represented in leadership literature? What about leadership roles?

   d. If women have been engaging in leadership practice well before formal leadership paradigms would suggest they were, what does this mean for our understanding of women and leadership?

   e. How can we disrupt the "leadership story most often told"?

5. *Conclusion* (5 minutes). The point of the activity is to illuminate how the most important things are not always the ones we hear about most readily. Instead, articulate how the stories most often told continue to perpetuate the dominant narrative.

Activity 3: Implicit Leadership Theory (40 minutes)
This activity invites participants to explore what implicit theory is and connect it to their individual experiences. Implicit theory "centers the importance of congruence between how people perceive leaders should be and how they actually show up" (Dugan, 2017, p. 9). These implicit theories are created through assumptions and socialization. In order to combat them, we must deconstruct and then reconstruct new possibilities.

1. *Preparation*. Project or provide an image of Dugan's (2017) table of reconstructed leadership theory clusters (p. 71).

2. *Introduction* (10 minutes). Have each participant take a minute and write or type the first five leaders that come to mind. Once everyone has done this, ask for participants to share their list and write the names on the board. After at least four participants have shared, request participants' observations about the list. Are there patterns in race, gender, socioeconomic status, ability, and other dimensions of identity? Students may need assistance in surfacing patterns. Make the connection that these patterns are reflective of how we have been socialized to define leaders and leadership.

3. *Group Conversation* (10 minutes). Connect that introductory activity to implicit theory and how something as simple as coming up with a list demonstrates the way people are socialized and assumptions we make about certain groups of people. Have participants highlight other leadership prototypes that have been prescribed to them about leadership (to see if they reflect dominant, masculine perspectives of leadership).

4. *Small Groups* (10 minutes). Have the participants choose a leadership cluster from the handout or projection and discuss why it resonates with them and how it connects to their lived experience.

5. *Large Group Synthesis* (10 minutes). Bring the groups back together and ask for volunteers to share. During this large group discussion connect their comments back to implicit theory. Wrap up this activity by asking participants to consider what it would look like for them to center themselves in all the identities they hold and to (re)imagine our

perceptions of leaders and leadership. Possible discussion questions:

a. Can you think of an instance when you were not perceived in a positive light as a leader? What was the circumstance?

b. How do your social identities influence your understanding and experience with implicit theory?

c. What are the benefits of interrogating our implicit leadership theories as we engage with leadership practice?

d. What are the potential pitfalls/challenges if we do not acknowledge our implicit leadership theories?

Facilitator Notes

Facilitators are encouraged to add questions that are specific to the group's context. This will help in making the experience relevant to your group. Participants' identities will impact how they experience this activity. The impact of social location on how participants

personally experience and know leadership can be part of the conversation.

References

Dugan, J. P. (2017). *Leadership theory: Cultivating critical perspectives*. Jossey-Bass.

Ely, R. J., Ibarra, H., & Kolb, D. M. (2011). Taking gender into account: Theory and design for women's leadership programs. *Academy of Management Learning & Education, 10,* 474–493. http://dx.doi.org/10.5465/amle.2010.0046

Biographies

Natasha T. Turman, PhD, is a visiting assistant professor for the Student Affairs in Higher Education (SAHE) program at Miami University.

Shamika KariKari, MS, is the associate director for the Office of Residence Life at Miami University and doctoral candidate in the SAHE program at Miami University.

SECTION TWO

Who Am I to Lead? The Role of Identity, Intersectionality, and Efficacy in Leadership Development

In this section, modules explore how identity, intersectionality, and efficacy impact women and leadership. Students explore both their personal (roles and responsibilities) and social (racial, cultural, religious, sexual, ableist, etc.) identities. They are also invited to consider the effects of interlocking systems of power, privilege, and oppression and how these forces shape their lives and multiple social identities. These modules invite both retrospective and future reflections and intention-setting.

Key Ideas

- Consciousness of self
- Self-authorship
- Self-efficacy
- Critical consciousness
- Intersectionality
- Leadership identity development

Developing Leadership Efficacy Through Critical Self-Reflection

Melissa Rocco

- Group size: ideally up to 20 people; if more than 20 people, divide participants into smaller groups with a facilitator for each one
- Time: 2–2.5 hours depending on group size and activity choices; the three parts could also be separated across three sessions
- Methods: large and small group discussion, drawing, reflective writing
- Materials: Blank legal-sized paper or larger (one sheet for each participant); markers, colored pencils, and crayons (shared among participants); pens (one per participant); tape
- Media: music for reflection while drawing

Overview

This three-part module is designed to help participants better understand the concepts of consciousness of self, self-authorship, and self-efficacy, as well as how those concepts relate to leadership broadly and in their own lives. Through drawing and reflective writing activities, participants will engage in critical self-reflection to better understand influences on their own leadership beliefs and their development of self-authorship and self-efficacy for leadership.

Learning Outcomes

- Increase understanding of consciousness of self, self-authorship, and self-efficacy; how they connect, differ, and matter to leadership
- Engage in critical self-reflection about how various experiences throughout one's life have contributed to one's beliefs about leadership
- Articulate one's leadership beliefs today and set meaningful intentions for future leadership practice

Direction

The three parts of this module build upon one another. They can be facilitated across several sessions or built into a longer workshop or retreat. Some aspects can be made longer or shorter to suit a particular context.

Part 1 – Clarifying Terms: A Small & Large Group Discussion (approximately 30 minutes)

1. *Small Groups* (10 minutes). If working with more than five participants, divide into small groups of four or five people. Ask participants to work together to come up with definitions for three concepts: consciousness of self, self-authorship, and self-efficacy. Share that the goal is to distinguish the difference among the

three concepts, so comparing and contrasting might be helpful. Let the groups know that they will report out to the larger group. Allow 5–10 minutes for the groups to work on their definitions. They may wish to have someone from the group take notes.

2. *Reporting Out & Concept Clarification* (10 minutes). Ask each group to report out their definitions. Facilitators should comment as groups report out regarding emergent themes across each group for each concept. Engage the large group in a conversation to clarify understanding of the three concepts.
   a. *Consciousness of Self* involves two aspects; (a) awareness and acknowledgement of one's personality and identities and (b) the ability to be a keen observer of your own actions, state of mind, emotions, and so on (HERI, 1996).
   b. *Self-authorship* involves the internal capacity to define one's own beliefs, identity, and interactions with others. It marks a shift from accepting knowledge from external influences/authorities without question or consideration toward constructing knowledge for oneself (Baxter Magolda & King, 2004).
   c. *Self-efficacy* involves one's internal belief regarding one's capacity to successfully engage in a particular task or action (Bandura, 2000).

3. *Large Group Conversation* (5–10 minutes). Ask the large group what connections can be made between these three concepts and leadership. Share the following ideas if not brought up in the discussion:
   a. *Regarding Consciousness of Self:* Developing our leadership understanding and practice requires us to engage in critical self-reflection (i.e., what we believe about leadership, why we believe it, how we have seen ourselves practice it in various situations, etc.; Rocco, 2017; Torrez & Rocco, 2015).
   b. *Regarding Self-authorship:* Self-authorship allows us to combine insight from our life and leadership experiences to determine what we believe about leadership (e.g.,

what leadership is, who it is for, how it happens, etc.) rather than relying on external sources to define leadership for us (Komives et al., 2009; Rocco, 2017).
   c. *Regarding Self-efficacy:* While a person may recognize their capacity (i.e., knowledge and skills) for leadership, whether or not they will take leadership action is determined by whether or not they believe in their ability to effectively engage in leadership (e.g., degree of leadership self-efficacy; Dugan, 2017; Holly et al., 2008).

Part 2 – Leadership Narratives Art Project (approximately 60 minutes)

1. *Preparation* (3 minutes). Set up the room and pass out materials: Provide a blank piece of legal-sized paper (or larger) and a pen to each participant. Place markers, colored pencils, and crayons around the room for participants to share. Share with participants that this is a creative drawing activity that will help them engage in critical self-reflection about the influence that various narratives about leadership we have heard throughout our lives have on our current leadership beliefs and practices; essentially examining the question "Why do we believe what we believe about leadership?" The facilitator will provide reflection prompts to guide participants' drawing. Play reflection music while participants are drawing.

2. *Individual Reflection and Drawing* (30–40 minutes). There are two questions; allow for 15–20 minutes for the first question before proceeding to the second one.
   a. Question 1: "What experiences throughout your life have influenced the way you think about leadership? Draw the people, places, symbols, or other reminders that represent those experiences."
   b. Question 2: "What leadership narratives (i.e., leadership lessons) were presented to you in each of the experiences in your drawing? What did the people in each experience believe about leadership? In what ways did people show leadership in each experience? What did each experience teach you about leadership?"

Ask participants to jot down notes on their drawing, on the back of their drawing, or on a separate sheet of paper, whichever option they prefer.

3. *Pair Share* (10 minutes). Ask participants to find a partner to share their reflections, identifying themes in the leadership narratives they have heard over time and making any relevant connections to culture, values, historical circumstances, social identities, and so forth. Partners should also discuss any commonalities and differences they see between their drawings and experiences. Ultimately, they should be reflecting on the original question "Why do we believe what we believe about leadership?"

4. *Gallery Walk* (5 minutes). Post artwork up in the room for everyone to see. Invite participants to mingle around the room to look at one another's drawings. This can be a verbal or nonverbal activity.

Part 3 – Setting Leadership Intentions (30–40 minutes)

1. *Introduction* (3 minutes). Share with participants that this is a short reflective writing activity that follows from the Leadership Narratives Art Project. This activity invites them to (a) determine and articulate what they believe about leadership today, and (b) set an intention (i.e., focus area, goal) for their leadership practice moving forward.

2. *Brief Individual Reflection* (5–10 minutes). Ask participants first to reflect on the following questions: "What is your leadership narrative today? What are the assumptions, beliefs, and ideas you have about leadership? How do you practice leadership at this point in your life?" Ask participants to write a short reflection (approximately 250–300 words) on this prompt, providing at least one recent example illustrating their current leadership practice.

3. *Choosing an Intention* (5 minutes). Ask participants to come up with a short statement (one or two sentences) that clearly articulates an intention for their leadership practice moving forward. Intentions are aspirational,

and often take the form of ideas a person wants to keep in mind, behaviors they want to try out, or an approach or perspective they wish to embrace. Participants' leadership intentions should connect in some way to their writing reflection. The point is to connect with their deeper leadership values and beliefs while embracing continual growth in their leadership understanding and practice.

4. *Large Group Share-Out* (10 minutes). Ask participants to share their intentions out loud with the large group. Share that the act of speaking intentions out into the world demonstrates commitment and can assist with accountability for participants to enact the intention.

Facilitator Notes

- While not everyone will consider themselves an artist, the act of drawing and coloring can be a powerful way to practice mindfulness and reflection. Reassure participants that the drawing can be true to life or abstract, a holistic picture or a series of separate drawings, whatever feels comfortable to each participant. The actions of drawing and coloring are just as important to the reflective process as what they draw to answer the prompt. Encourage participants to take up the time provided and really tap into their creative sides. This is also why providing larger paper and ample art materials (markers, colored pencils, crayons, etc.) is important; these items further encourage creativity.

- Set the expectation that if participants finish early at any point during the drawing activity, they should sit quietly so as to not interrupt the process of any of the other participants.

- The writing reflection in Part 3 can be done in the session, in a subsequent session, or for homework. If there is not time for intentions to be shared out loud to the large group, they can be posted online to a group discussion board. Participants may also wish to write their intention on their drawing somewhere.

References

Bandura, A. (2000). Exercise of human agency through collective efficacy. *Current Directions in Psychological Science, 9*(3), 75–78.

Baxter Magolda, M., and King, P. M. (2004). *Learning partnerships: Theory and models of practice to educate for self-authorship*. Stylus.

Dugan, J. P. (2017). *Leadership theory: Building critical perspectives*. Jossey-Bass.

Higher Education Research Institute. (1996). *A social change model of leadership development guidebook* (Version III).

Holly, S. T., Avolio, B. J., Luthans, F., & Harms, P. D. (2008). Leadership efficacy: Review and future directions. *Leadership Quarterly, 19*, 669–692.

Komives, S. R., Longerbeam, S., Mainella, F. C., Osteen, L., & Owen, J. E. (2009). Leadership identity development: Challenges in applying a developmental model. *Journal of Leadership Education, 8*(1), 11–47.

Rocco, M. L. (2017). *Moving beyond common paradigms of leadership: Understanding the development of advanced leadership identity* [Doctoral dissertation] (Publication No. 10285840). ProQuest Dissertations and Theses.

Torrez, M. A., & Rocco, M. L. (2015). Building critical capacities for leadership learning. In J. E. Owen (Ed.), *Innovative learning for leadership development* (New Directions for Student Leadership, no. 145, pp. 19–34). Jossey-Bass.

Biography

Melissa Rocco, PhD, serves as lecturer and coordinator for leadership studies and affiliate assistant professor in the Department of Counseling, Higher Education, and Special Education at the University of Maryland.

The Puzzle of Predecessors, Instigators, and Inheritors

Katherine Quigley

- Group size: Any
- Time: 40 minutes
- Methods: group discussion, groups, independent work
- Materials needed: Copies of Predecessors, Instigators, and Inheritors Puzzle Pieces (one set per student), scissors, and pencil

---

Overview

Leadership literature suggests that predecessors, instigators, and inheritors influence ideas and experiences of gender and leadership (Owen, 2020). By examining the role of those who have previously advocated for gender equity (predecessors), those who are currently fighting for women/gender-related issues (instigators), or those who will emerge in the future (inheritors) participants can learn about themselves and the movements and values that are important to them. Exploring the connectedness among these three is vital when examining gender justice in leadership. This exercise is a personal puzzle that invites students to put together their leadership predecessors, instigators, and inheritors. It can be done with any number of participants.

Learning Outcomes

- Identify individuals who are their predecessors, instigators, and inheritors. Include examples, reasoning for each, and how they directly influence them
- Understand how leadership intersects with everyday effects on their goals, decisions, and paths

Directions

1. *Introduction* (5 minutes). Introduce the idea of predecessors, instigators, and inheritors and briefly provide an example of the three puzzle pieces. Distribute a set of three puzzle pieces to each person.
2. *Independent Work* (10 minutes). Invite students to work independently to complete each puzzle piece.
3. *Pair Share* (10 minutes). Working in pairs, students will share their predecessors, instigators, and inheritors.
4. *Group Debrief* (15 minutes). The aim of the debrief is to help students see how their

own sense of self and leadership is shaped by predecessors, instigators, and inheritors, and how individual and collective exercise of leadership means working in continuous collaboration with those before, during, and after our time.

a. What influenced or guided your choice of who to assign to the puzzle pieces?

b. Do you think they would think of themselves in this way?

c. How does each piece connect to tell the story of your leadership?

d. What piece of the puzzle might you be for someone else?

e. Think of how the predecessors, instigators, and inheritors connect; how does this shift your thoughts on we impact others' leadership?

Facilitator Notes

- Facilitators should be prepared to offer examples of their own puzzle pieces.
- Participants may find it difficult to identify predecessors, instigators, and inheritors in

their personal lives. In this case, remind them that leadership is both informal and formal. If they continue to struggle, have them consider someone who has been an influential leader in society. For example, Ellen DeGeneres, as an entertainer and leader, has been a predecessor to countless leaders who she has influenced. Ellen was an instigator for LGBTQ+ visibility and rights in the 1997 coming out episode of her sitcom. In addition, she would identify her mother as an inspiration and a source of support.

Reference

Owen, J. E. (2020). *We are the leaders we've been waiting for: Women and leadership development in college.* Stylus.

Biography

Katherine Quigley is a teacher in Fairfax County Public Schools (Virginia); she has a BA in special education with a minor in leadership studies from George Mason University.

Handout 2.2.1 The Puzzle of Predecessors, Instigators, & Inheritors

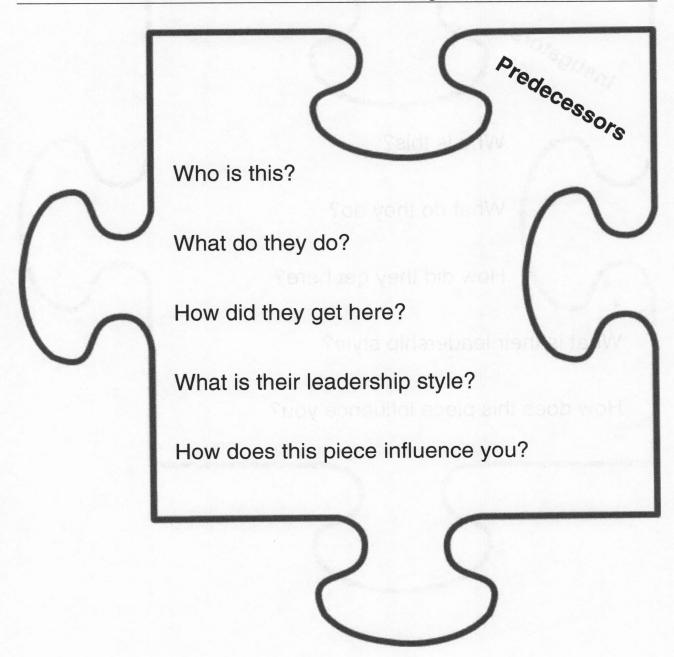

Predecessors

Who is this?

What do they do?

How did they get here?

What is their leadership style?

How does this piece influence you?

Instigators

Who is this?

What do they do?

How did they get here?

What is their leadership style?

How does this piece influence you?

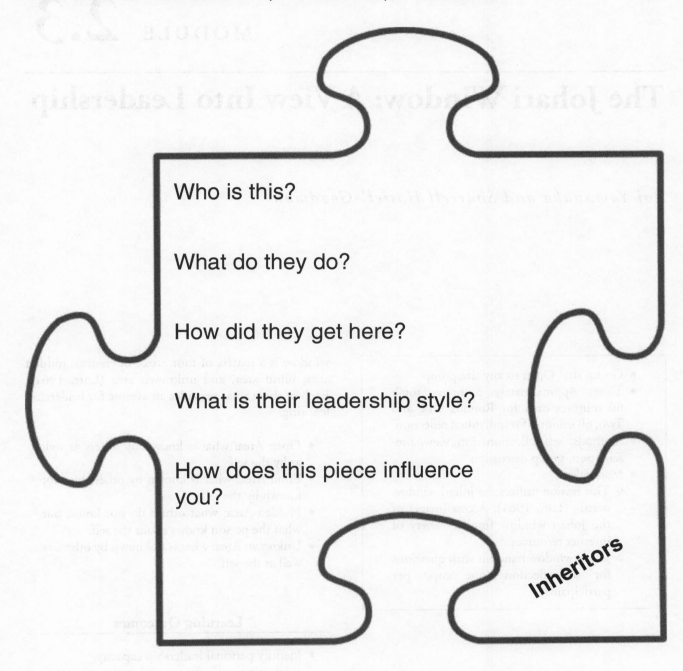

Who is this?

What do they do?

How did they get here?

What is their leadership style?

How does this piece influence you?

Inheritors

The Johari Window: A View Into Leadership

Aoi Yamanaka and Sharrell Hassell-Goodman

- Group size: Open to any size group
- Time: Approximately 3 hours total: 60 minutes each for Rounds One and Two; 60 minutes for individual reflection.
- Methods: self-reflection, interview, presentation, group discussion
- Materials:
  - This session utilizes the Johari window matrix (Luft, 1961). Access images of the Johari window from a variety of internet resources.
  - Johari window handout with questions for self-reflection (one copy per participant).

window is a matrix of four areas: open area, hidden area, blind area, and unknown area (Luft, 1961). Each of these areas provides an avenue for leadership learning.

- Open Area: what is known by others as well as by the self.
- Blind Area: what is known by others but not known by the self.
- Hidden Area: what others do not know, but what the person knows about the self.
- Unknown Area: what is unknown by others as well as the self.

Learning Outcomes

- Identify personal leadership capacity, motivation, self-efficacy, and enactment
- Interpret own leadership capacity, motivation, self-efficacy, and enactment that are not recognized by oneself and others
- Analyze own leadership efficacy as an important moderator between leadership capacity and enactment
- Evaluate areas for leadership growth and development
- Develop future plans for leadership growth and continuous leadership engagement

Overview

Participants will assess their own development of leadership capacity, motivation, self-efficacy, and enactment; they will also reflect on their leadership efficacy as an important moderator between leadership capacity and enactment. This activity is based on the concept of the Johari window, which was developed by Luft and Ingham as a model of interpersonal awareness (Luft, 1961). The Johari

Directions

Round One (60 minutes)

1. *Preparation.* Draw on the board or project onto the wall an image of the Johari window.

2. *Introduction of Johari Window* (10 minutes). Review the concept of the Johari window. Describe the four quadrants and use a personal example to illustrate the four quadrants and how this is a tool for deepening understanding and practice. Connect the Johari window to leadership learning, specifically leadership ability, motivation, self-efficacy, and enactment. Remind participants that leadership can take place in multiple ways, not only as a formal position, but in the classroom, at work, and within family and friend groups; all types of leadership are honored in this activity.

3. *Personal Reflection & Pair Share* (25 minutes). Distribute the reflection guide and invite students to individually reflect on the "Open Area" and write some answers to the questions. Before shifting students into individual work, remind them of your "Open Area" reflections. After about 10 minutes of individual reflection, invite students to form pairs and share their responses.

4. *Large Group Synthesis* (15 minutes). Return to the large group and invite participants to share about their experience of the first quadrant. During this sharing out, the facilitator can gauge how well the students understand the Johari window and how the questions call them to understand their leadership more deeply.

5. *Next Steps* (10 minutes). Provide participants with time to complete the self-reflection and engage in interviews to help complete the Blind Area. Ask students to bring their written notes and reflections to the next session.

Round Two (50 minutes)

6. *Johari Window: A Second Look* (10 minutes). Remind students of the purpose of this exercise and connect it explicitly to leadership learning and development related to leadership ability, motivation, self-efficacy, and enactment. Explore what those terms mean and connect them to how they might show up in the Johari window exercise. Use examples to make the ideas concrete.

7. *Trios* (20 minutes). Invite students to form trios and review the results of their Johari window reflections. Ask that each student be given 5 minutes to speak about their four quadrants while the other trio members listen. After each person has shared, then the group can offer comments and questions to each other. In their final comments to each other, ask students to share what is one question about their own leadership that emerged after listening to their peers.

8. *Large Group Debrief* (15 minutes). During the final large group debrief, facilitators can invite participants to consider concretely a comparison of their self-reflections with what their interviewees shared.

   a. What was it like for you to engage in the activity—to examine yourself, to ask others for feedback, to be interviewed about others, to share your insights in the trio?

   b. What did you learn about yourself and your leadership? What surprised you?

   c. What was encouraging or discouraging about this exercise?

   d. Which questions or aspects of this exercise challenge you the most?

   e. What excites you in your leadership learning?

   f. What motivates you in your exercise of leadership?

   g. How will you apply this to your leadership ability, motivation, self-efficacy, and enactment? What are your next concrete steps?

9. *Statement of Intent* (5 minutes). Jumping from that final question, invite students to craft a statement of intent, a leadership goal that they develop as a result of the insights and knowledge gained through the Johari window exercise. The facilitator can share an example from their own leadership journey. Ask students to write this statement of intent in a place where it can serve as a reminder. Invite them to see the Johari window as a tool that can provide insights over time.

Facilitator Notes

This activity includes three movements: introduction, individual time for reflection and interviews, and large group synthesis. These movements can happen within one longer session or split across two sessions. The facilitator may need to modify expectations about the number of interviews if the session occurs in one large block of time.

Facilitators of this module need to have a good grasp of the Johari window and its application to leadership learning and development.

- Leadership self-efficacy refers to "individuals' belief in the likelihood they will be successful when engaging in leadership" (Dugan & Correia, 2014, p. 25).
- Leadership motivation is one's motivation to lead, including attending leadership training, roles, and responsibilities (Dugan, 2017).
- Leadership capacity reflects one's knowledge, skills, and abilities related to the leader role or leadership process (Dugan, 2017).
- Leadership enactment "is when capacity is put into action or the functional practice of leadership. It is the behaviors of an individual or group as they engage in leader role or leadership processes" (Dugan, 2017, p. 14).

Finally, the facilitator should remind participants that directed and deep reflection—particularly about

unknown areas—can evoke memories and emotions, sometimes unexpectedly. Encourage students' self-care throughout the process and be prepared with resources that can provide professional assistance, such as counseling.

References

Dugan, J. P. (2017). *Leadership theory: Cultivating critical perspectives.* Jossey-Bass.

Dugan, J. P., & Correia, B. (2014). *MSL insight report supplement: Leadership program delivery.* National Clearinghouse for Leadership Programs.

Luft, J. (1961). The Johari window: A graphic model of awareness in interpersonal relations. *NTL Human Relations Training News,* 5(1), 6–7. https://docuri.com/download/the-johari-window-a-graphic-model_59c1d45cf581710b2865a986_pdf

Biographies

Aoi Yamanaka, PhD, is a term assistant professor and associate director of academic services in the School of Integrative Studies at George Mason University.

Sharrell Hassell-Goodman is a full time doctoral student at George Mason University pursuing a degree in higher education with a concentration in women and gender studies and social justice.

Handout 2.3.1: The Johari Window: A View Into Leadership

The Johari window is a model that provides a mechanism for learning more about oneself. This tool is helpful in gaining self-awareness and personal development within the leadership context. The following questions provide an opportunity to engage in exploration of self and reflect on how one is perceived by others. Since this is the Johari window and a view within your leadership, we are asking you to consider the open, blind, hidden, and unknown areas in your leadership.

Open Area

The open area is information that is easily obtainable and known by the person ("the self") and known by others ("others"). This includes behaviors, attitudes, emotions, knowledge, experience, skills, and point of view. Reflect on the following questions and write a brief summary that describes your open area. You do not need to answer each of these questions; rather, use them to help you discover more about your open area.

1. *Primary Questions*
   a. What motivates your leadership?
   b. What keeps you engaged or makes you do what you do as a leader?
   c. What are your leadership abilities?
2. *Secondary Questions*
   a. What are some of your experiences in formal roles and/or active involvements on campus and/or in the community?
   b. Reflect on an experience of accomplishing tasks (as a leader) that reduced self-doubt or strengthened previous experiences. What did you learn about yourself as a result?
   c. Who is your role model? Why? What positive influence/impacts has the person had on you?
   d. How have you been acknowledged as a leader? What have you been known to do as a leader?
   e. How have you struggled with your leadership journey? What psychological

and emotional impacts did you experience from your struggle? How have they changed your leadership?
   f. How do you demonstrate your leadership? What makes you a leader?

Summary Reflection: How Open Is Your Leadership to Yourself and Others?

Blind Area

The blind area is information about yourself that you are not aware of but that others recognize. This is particularly true in group settings. You may be naive about the way your leadership impacts others. Over time, this area will become smaller as you learn how your leadership is perceived by others.

In addition to answering the following questions for yourself, interview others who know your leadership capacity (one's knowledge and skills related to leadership), enactment (capacity is put into action), self-efficacy (belief in likelihood to be successful), and motivation (motivation to lead). Be sure to ask people who can give you honest and constructive feedback. Try to ask people who know you in different settings (mentor, friend, family member, supervisor, professor, coworker, etc.). This is not about revealing your deepest secrets but rather an opportunity to identify areas of growth and concrete examples of how they see you exercise leadership.

1. *Primary Questions*
   a. How did others in your group describe your leadership?
   b. How have others misunderstood and/or appreciated your leadership skills and capability?
   c. How have others misunderstood or made assumptions about your leadership because of your identities and/or culture?

2. *Secondary Questions*
   a. What is the difference between your leadership intention versus your impact? For example, are you sometimes misunderstood or do people interpret your leadership in ways that were unintended?
   b. How does this impact your leadership? What are those blind spots as a result?
   c. What constructive feedback have you received about your leadership? What kind of feedback serves as a distraction? How has this in turn helped you grow as a leader?
   d. What are you capable of doing well and in what areas can others help you grow?

3. *Interview Questions (to ask others about you)*
   a. What are some potential hidden talents, traits, characteristics or skill sets that you think I possess and can also develop?
   b. What are some experiences or opportunities for self-discovery that I need to take advantage of in order to develop as a leader?
   c. What observations have you made about me that you think impacts my ability as a

leader? What opportunities for growth and moments of success do you think I should be aware of? What should I cultivate and what should I do more of?
   d. Do you have any advice for me on how I could continue to believe in myself, my ability to accomplish tasks, and my overall leadership?

Summary Reflection: What Are Your Blind Spots and How Might You Address Them?

---

   e. What is a hidden gem that I possess? What do you think I don't recognize or believe about myself that is good, excellent, or worth noting?

Hidden Area

The hidden area is information that you keep hidden from others. This includes true feelings, hidden agenda, secrets, past experiences, and private information that might influence the group. This section can be only completed by individual self-reflection. Ask yourself:

1. What are your hidden fears about leadership and what keeps them hidden? How does your fear influence your leadership capacity, motivation, self-efficacy, and enactment?
2. What do you hide from others regarding your leadership?
   a. What about leadership makes you nervous, afraid, or feel small?
   b. When there are hidden areas, they limit your growth; for example, have you had moments in your leadership that created misunderstandings, poor communication, or confusion? How does this then demonstrate your limitations?
3. How does your identity impact what you keep hidden or what you show readily?
4. How are you becoming aware of hidden information that is impacting your ability to grow as a leader?

Summary Reflection: What Are Some Hidden Areas in Your Leadership That You Are Now Motivated to Change?

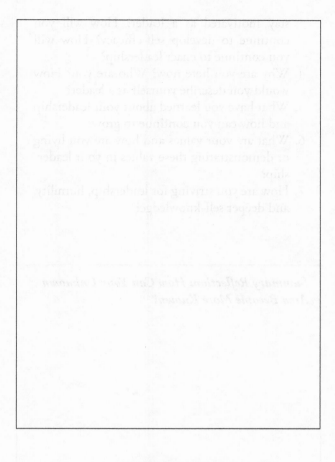

Unknown Area

This quadrant is information, feelings, capabilities, talents and strengths, and so forth that are unknown to the self and others. The unknown item can be the result of many things, including repressed emotions, gifts and talents that have not yet surfaced, long-term patterns of behavior and thought, or skills and aptitudes that are currently underdeveloped or underappreciated. This area remains unknown until you engage in exploration and discovery. The only way to expand your unknown area is to engage in deep reflections by yourself and have deep conversations with others. Reflect on the following questions:

1. How do you envision your future leadership, both formal and informal?
2. How do you keep engaging in these opportunities to continue developing your unknown area?
3. How do you continue to develop your capacity for leadership? How will you continue to

stay motivated as a leader? How will you continue to develop self-efficacy? How will you continue to enact leadership?

4. Why are you here now? Who are you? How would you describe yourself as a leader?
5. What have you learned about your leadership and how can you continue to grow?
6. What are your values and how are you living or demonstrating these values in your leadership?
7. How are you striving for leadership, humility, and deeper self-knowledge?

Summary Reflection: How Can Your Unknown Area Become More Known?

MODULE **2.4**

Identity and Intersectionality in Leadership

Arnèle Francis and Rukan Said

- Group size: 10–20 people
- Estimated time: 50 minutes
- Materials: two readings (Clark-Taylor, 2017; and Moradi & Grzanka, 2017); large paper and markers

---

Overview

This module contains two activities in which students explore the theory of intersectionality and interrogate what leadership can look like through the lens of intersectionality. Students will use two readings to explore their own multiple identities and investigate the ways in which these identities shape their experiences of sameness and difference with others. Moreover, this activity is meant to strengthen their understanding of how interlocking systems of privilege and oppression interact with their multiple identities and affect their self-efficacy and leadership.

Learning Outcomes

- Strengthen understanding of critical self-analysis
- Deepen understandings of dominant narratives and how they manifest and are reinforced

- Consider the social contexts within which some individuals are disenfranchised and others are empowered
- Understand how socialization influences how we see and experience the world
- Explore strategies for incorporating mindfulness and reflection into leadership practices

Directions

Activity Option One

1. *Preparation.* All students should receive physical copies of or electronic access to Clark-Taylor (2017) and Moradi and Gzranka (2017) and be instructed to read them in advance of the session.
2. *Generate Key Themes* (10 minutes). At the beginning of the session, work with students to generate key themes and ideas from the readings. This establishes a basis for the written reflection.
3. *Written Reflection* (15 minutes). Allow students 15 minutes to respond to the following reflection questions:
   a. How is intersectionality different from having multiple identities?
   b. What are the intersections that you experience? What privileged or oppressed identities do you hold?

c. How do these intersections inform your sense of self-efficacy around leadership?

d. In what ways can you leverage your experiences of intersectional oppression or privilege into your leadership approach? How or why?

e. What was the most poignant thing you learned about intersectionality in the readings that you were not aware of before? Why?

4. *Pair-Share* (10 minutes). Invite students to talk in pairs about their responses.

5. *Group Debrief* (25 minutes). Work through each reflection question, allowing students to offer their responses, and then step back for new insights and questions.

Activity Option Two

1. *Preparation.* All students should receive physical copies of or electronic access to the Clark-Taylor (2017) and Moradi and Gzranka (2017). Divide the group into two and have each half read one of the readings.

2. *Small Groups* (20 minutes). Upon arrival to the session, divide the students into small groups based on which reading they encountered, approximately four or five students per small group. Distribute large paper and markers to each group. Allow students 15 minutes to discuss the readings and generate their main points in relation to these discussion questions:

   a. How does self-reflection help to fuel effective leadership?

   b. How do power and normativity interact to validate certain forms of leadership? Why?

   c. What does it mean to have and maintain an intersectional approach to leadership? Why?

   d. How do power and normativity interact to create and sustain oppressive mechanisms within society?

   e. How do privilege and positionality impact interpersonal relationships?

3. *Presentation of Findings* (15 minutes). Each team will then present their findings and entertain questions and comments from the students who read the other article.

4. *Final Debrief* (15 minutes). Reflective discussion, as a class, led by the facilitator. The aim

is that students critically think about leadership through an intersectional lens, in the ways that it can be restricted and upheld, in relation to their various identities. Students are encouraged to use the readings on intersectionality to illuminate their understandings of their own multiple identities and interrogate the relationship of these identities to their own ideas around leadership and self-efficacy.

Facilitator Notes

This activity is not meant to strictly define leadership and intersectionality. Rather, it is meant to push students in the direction of beginning to recognize the benefits of including intersectionality in their understanding of leadership. At the heart of leadership is inclusivity. Thus, as students reflect on their own leadership styles and methods, this activity should encourage them to adopt an intersectional lens to grow their leadership development and leadership identity.

References

Clark-Taylor, A. (2017). Developing critical consciousness and social justice self-efficacy: Lessons from feminist community engagement student narratives. *Journal of Higher Education Outreach and Engagement, 21*(4), 81–115. https://files.eric.ed.gov/fulltext/EJ1163711.pdf

Moradi, B., & Grzanka, P. R. (2017). Using intersectionality responsibly: Toward critical epistemology, structural analysis, and social justice activism. *Journal of Counseling Psychology, 64*(5), 500–513. https://psycnet.apa.org/doi/10.1037/cou0000203

Biographies

Arnèle Francis is a proud Black woman from the twin-island federation of St. Kitts and Nevis; she has a BA in Integrative Studies with a concentration in Legal Studies, and minors in Women and Gender Studies and Social Justice from George Mason University and plans to pursue law.

Rukan Said is a Black feminist scholar, facilitator, writer, and speaker.

Leadership Identity Development: Letter to My Future Self

Erika Cohen Derr

- Group size: This activity can be done with any size group, but small- to medium-sized groups may promote deeper conversation and insight
- Time: 90 minutes, distributed over two sessions separated by several months or one year. Session 1, 45 minutes; Session 2, 45 minutes
- Methods: Individual reflection, writing, small group discussion, large group discussion
- Materials: Paper, envelope, writing instrument (or computers/printers)

Overview

The leadership identity development (LID) theory and model seek to address the question of how individuals develop a leadership identity in the context of the social experience of working purposefully toward change (Komives et al., 2005, 2006, 2009). Applying LID theory invites reflection about whether and how leadership serves as an identity. As such, the theory implies that, as an identity, leadership serves as both a role with characteristics, social relationships, and memberships, and also as a lens through which experiences

are interpreted and imbued with meaning (Oyserman et al., 2012). This activity provides an opportunity to reflect on personal past assumptions, beliefs, and expectations and examine how one has changed in one's understanding, views, and self-regard.

Learning Outcomes

- Apply foundational leadership concepts to personal experience
- Evaluate how personal experiences promote deeper awareness of leadership concepts
- Examine personal understanding of the differences between the constructions of "leader" and "leadership"

Directions

Session 1 (45 minutes)

1. *Letter Writing* (30 minutes). Provide participants with paper and ask them to write a letter to their future self about their leadership experiences this year. Inform participants before the assignment whether the final written reflection is for their use only, or if the facilitator will review it. Share the following prompt:

a. Main prompt: Write a letter to yourself in the future to imagine and describe the ways that you will grow and evolve as a leader this year. Imagine something that you expect to happen on this leadership journey. Use descriptive language to predict what you might encounter, experience, or feel.

b. What is your main objective or purpose? How will you focus your leadership energy this year or term?

c. How does "who you are" influence how you lead? Which parts of your identity are most important to you? In what ways do your identities inform your leadership priorities and practice?

d. What strengths do you bring to your leadership role(s)? Where do you experience the greatest challenge? What growth do you expect in yourself?

e. How do you face resistance or pressure in your leadership efforts? What strategies do you use to manage this type of opposition or stress?

f. Who are the people that work with you and support you in these efforts? What do you contribute to those relationships? What do those relationships need from you?

g. What is it like to work with other people? How do you prefer to contribute? What do you need and value from others?

2. *Debrief* (10 minutes). Provide participants sufficient time to write the letter. Invite students to reflect out loud about the experience of letter writing.

a. What was it like to sit and write to yourself for 30 minutes?

b. What questions seemed hard or easy to answer?

c. On what will you focus your leadership energy this semester or term, and how might this group be supportive?

d. What do you imagine might happen in your leadership journey across this next period of time?

e. How might you continue to be attentive to your leadership practice moving forward?

3. *Closing* (3 minutes). At the end of the conversation, have each participant place the letter in an envelope with their name on it and seal it closed. Let students know that you will store the letters securely for the duration of the group experience, up to one year.

Session 2 (45 minutes)

1. *Individual Reading* (10 minutes). After time has passed and the group has reconvened, return the letters to the participants. Ask them to open the sealed envelope and read the letter to themselves. Invite them to take a few notes about their initial response to reading the letter.

2. *Pairs or Trios* (15 minutes). Divide the group into smaller groups of two or three. Ask participants to discuss in small groups using the following questions:

a. When you read your letter from the beginning of the experience, what stands out to you?

b. Did your purpose or focus hold true? How were you able to effect this change this year? Where or how did you encounter resistance in your leadership efforts?

c. How did your hypotheses hold up? What was as you expected or predicted? What surprised you? What does this say about your understanding of leadership?

d. What was your emotional reaction to this letter? How did it make you feel to read your words and imagination?

e. How have your beliefs and assumptions about leadership changed in the time that you wrote this letter?

f. What do you understand more clearly now than you did when you wrote the letter? What seems more confusing or uncertain?

g. How do your reactions compare with each other? Did anyone have a distinctly similar or distinctly different reaction or experience?

3. *Large Group Debrief* (20 minutes). When small groups have explored these questions, bring the large group back together and ask participants to share key insights with the large

group. To connect these reflections back to the core concept of leadership, ask students to reflect in writing on the following questions:

a. How has your understanding of leadership changed since you first wrote this letter? How has your understanding of yourself changed?

b. Think about the beliefs that you currently hold about leadership. Write down three things that you believe. What seems indelible, or unchangeable, to you? What belief might you interrogate more deeply? Do any concepts lead you to question something you once thought was unchangeable?

Facilitator Notes

1. In order to make letter writing more immersive and complete, create a handout with these questions in a list. Or, create a multipage handout that visually represents these questions in bubbles, squares, or other shapes that help the student make sure to address them all.

2. The activity can be modified based on time and group conditions. One modification is to provide the initial assignment several weeks in advance of a group meeting, for example, upon registering for a class or upon beginning a new leadership role like a resident assistant.

3. If the nature of the experience is such that the group will not be able to reconvene after an extended period and process the activity as an intact group, the activity may be modified to prompt participants to reflect on an experience from the past and debrief about the ways their views have changed. The activity relies on the experience of shifting perspectives between present and future, or past and present, to highlight the changing view of self in relation to core concepts of relational leadership and leadership as identity.

4. If relevant to the group experience, the facilitator may share information about the LID theory and model, highlighting Stage Three (Leader Identified) and Stage Four (Leadership

Differentiated). This is particularly relevant if participants reflect actively on the changing view of other people as leaders, and on their relationships with others as reciprocal.

5. Similarly, if relevant to the group, the facilitator may explain the concept of "orders of consciousness" presented in Kegan (1994) and describe the "subject–object" shift that occurs when experience is later interpreted to have meaning that was not evident at the time, and prompts one to see themselves and others with a different, enlarged perspective. Participants could be asked to share examples to illustrate their changed view of themselves or of leadership.

Additional Background

The LID theory draws upon the work of psychologist Robert Kegan (1994) in crafting development as a set of stages characterized by periods of stability and periods of disequilibrium (Komives et al., 2005, 2006). Kegan (1994) describes "Orders of Consciousness"—similar to stages—used to organize, make sense of, and draw meaning from the experience of the self in the world (pp. 94–95). In the LID theory and model, this shift underscores the particular transition when one encounters the change from positional, or role-based, constructions of leadership to relational, or process-based, considerations of leadership (Komives et al., 2005, 2006). Applying the LID model to women's leadership development offers the chance to consider the influence of gender on leadership. Examining the shift between Stage Three, Leader Identified, and Stage Four, Leadership Differentiated, in particular, offers rich context for considering how gender may influence one's interpretation of experiences and one's assessment of leadership as an identity.

References

Kegan, R. (1994). *In over our heads: The mental demands of modern life*. Harvard University Press.

Komives, S. R., Longerbeam, S., Mainella, F., Osteen, L., & Owen, J. (2009). Leadership identity development:

Challenges in applying a developmental model. *Journal of Leadership Education, 8*, 11–47. https://pdfs.semanticscholar.org/f1a7/6907f39ac90734ee07059e79b4cc3707ba44.pdf

Komives, S. R., Longerbeam, S., Owen, J., Mainella, F., & Osteen, L. (2006). A leadership identity development model: Applications from a grounded theory. *Journal of College Student Development, 47*, 401–418. https://www.researchgate.net/deref/http%3A%2F%2Fdx.doi.org%2F10.1353%2Fcsd.2006.0048.

Komives, S. R., Owen, J., Longerbeam, S., Mainella, F., & Osteen, L. (2005). Developing a leadership identity: A grounded theory. *Journal of College Student Development, 46*, 593–611. https://www.researchgate.net/deref/http%3A%2F%2Fdx.doi.org%2F10.1353%2Fcsd.2005.0061.

Oyserman, D., Elmore, K., & Smith, G. (2012). Self, self-concept, and identity. In M. Leary and J. P. Tangney (Eds.), *Handbook of self and identity* (pp. 69–104). Guilford Press.

Biography

Erika Cohen Derr, DLS, is assistant vice president of student affairs at Georgetown University, where she focuses on student engagement and leadership development.

How Did We Get Here? How Gender Socialization Shapes Women in Leadership

In this section you will find modules that explore the way social, cultural, political, individual, and organizational dynamics shape the developmental experiences of girls and women. Concepts such as the Ophelia complex of postpubescent girls (Pipher, 1994), chilly classroom climates, queen bees and wannabes (Wiseman, 2009), crises of confidence, and leadership biases are presented. Issues of sexuality, appearance, and media influence are also addressed. Students are encouraged not only rewrite a fairy tale; they also trace their own gender journeys.

Key Ideas

- Gender socialization
- Cycle of socialization
- Media representation of gender

References

Pipher, M. (1994). *Reviving Ophelia: Saving the selves of adolescent girls.* Riverhead Books.

Wiseman, R. (2016). *Queen bees and wannabes: Helping your daughter survive cliques, gossip, boys, and the new realities of girl world* (3rd ed.). Harmony Books.

MODULE **3.1**

Key Concepts of Gender Socialization and Media Influences

Paige Haber-Curran and Grisell Pérez-Carey

- Group size: any size
- Time: 90 minutes (modifications can allow for 40+ minutes; see suggestions in Facilitator Notes)
- Methods: Presentation of information, small group activity, large group discussion and debrief
- Materials: Copies of Key Concepts of Gender Socialization handout (one per participant); large flip chart paper (enough for one sheet per group of five to seven participants plus a few extra); markers (enough for two markers per group of five to seven participants)

Overview

In this module participants examine key concepts of gender socialization that affect girls and young women with a focus on messages from media platforms. Participants will review and discuss key gender socialization concepts and examine these concepts alongside article titles and topics included in various media platforms targeting adolescent girls and young women; they will identify how the different titles and topics may reinforce or challenge these concepts.

The module concludes with participants developing content for a media platform of their choosing that includes articles and topics that can help combat these gender socialization issues.

Learning Outcomes

- Identify and describe key concepts of gender socialization affecting girls and young women, such as: effortless perfection, imposter syndrome, Ophelia complex, crisis of confidence, gendered leadership biases, queen bees and wannabes, and chilly classroom climate
- Critically analyze titles included in various media platforms targeting adolescent girls and young women through the lens of gender socialization concepts
- Construct content for a media platform that can help combat gender socialization issues facing girls and young women

Directions

1. *Review of Key Concepts* (10 minutes). Facilitator begins with discussing gender socialization and reviewing key concepts using

the Key Concepts of Gender Socialization handout. In discussing the key concepts, introduce intersectionality and stress that while these concepts focus on gender, other identities intersect with gender and can play a salient role in individuals' socialization and experiences. Ask participants how popular media platforms may contribute to each of the gender socialization concepts introduced.

2. *Small Group Work* (15 minutes). In groups of five to seven, have participants as a group or individually examine media platforms that are frequently viewed by girls and young women. Participants should identify article titles or topics that relate to the key concepts of gender socialization that may contribute to or combat the gender socialization concepts. Popular platforms may include social media sites (e.g., Instagram, Twitter, Facebook, Snapchat), social media hashtags, magazines (e-magazines and print), blogs, Pinterest, television, news outlets, and so on. Refer to the Examples of Media Platforms and Article Titles handout at the end of this module as needed; it may be helpful to select a few of these to share as examples with the group. Participants will connect articles and topics that they identify to the key concepts in gender socialization by jotting down notes in the third column of the Key Concepts of Gender Socialization handout.

3. *Large Group Conversation* (15 minutes). After participants have applied the key concepts to their examples, bring the group together as a large group and ask for examples for each concept. Ask participants:
   a. How do these examples reinforce or combat the key concepts?
   b. In what ways are these concepts internalized by media consumers?
   c. How have these examples distorted their or others' views of girls and women in leadership, in terms of things such as roles, approaches, aspirations, and efficacy?
   d. How do concepts of gender socialization play out in popular culture?

4. *Small Group Work* (20 minutes). Now instruct the small groups to develop new content (e.g., article titles, photo gallery suggestions, quiz or interview topics, or other content) for a media platform of their choosing to combat the key gender socialization concepts and empower girls and young women. Encourage them to include content that acknowledges women's intersectional identities. Pass out flip chart paper and markers to each group, and instruct them to write the content on the flip chart paper to share with other groups.

5. *Gallery Experience* (10+ minutes). Upon completion, instruct each group to hang their flip chart paper where it is visible for the group to see. Invite participants to move through the room to see what other groups created; or, provide each group with 2 or 3 minutes to present their content to the large group.

6. *Large Group Debrief* (20 minutes). After participants have seen or heard the new media content, lead a large group debrief centered on the way media platforms contribute to the manifestation of the key gender socialization concepts and ways that we can combat those concepts. Encourage participants to think about gender broadly and women's leadership more specifically and to be action-oriented in their responses. Invite them to think critically about the concepts of gender socialization and ways these concepts continue to appear in media, contribute to gender socialization, and/or manifest in their daily lives within their classrooms, organizations, and so forth. In discussing ways that media reinforce and/or combat the concepts, there is an opportunity to discuss purchasing power. Purchasing power, like many of the other discussion topics included in this module, can be examined in an intersectional manner. Some discussion/debrief topics/questions include:
   a. In what ways have you seen a shift in media content over the years?
   b. What media platforms, companies, celebrities/influencers, or sites align with your newly constructed content?
   c. In what ways does your media intake make you complicit to the negative concepts? In what ways does your media intake combat the negative concepts?

d. How can you actively combat these key concepts through your actions and encourage others to do the same?

e. How can we empower girls and young women in leadership?

Facilitator Notes

Modifications of the activity can include the following:

- The facilitator can find examples via various media sources for students to analyze and apply the concepts. Prior to doing so, the facilitator can create a poll or ask students what media platforms they currently or previously read or viewed. This could provide insight into what messaging students receive.
- If there is not enough time to do the full module, the first three parts of the module (approximately 40 minutes) could be completed together as a group and participants could complete the remaining three components as a take-home assignment or virtually.
- Depending on group size and/or time, it may be beneficial for the small groups to discuss the debrief questions prior to coming together with the large group to allow participant engagement in both small and large groups. Additionally, this could allow groups to engage in a deeper level of dialogue on the concepts.

References

Clance, P. R., & Imes, S. (1978). The imposter phenomenon in high achieving women: Dynamics and therapeutic intervention. *Psychotherapy: Theory, Research, and Practice, 15*(3), 241–247.

Duke University. (2003). *Women's initiative report.* The Women's Initiative. http://universitywomen.stanford.edu/reports/WomensInitiativeReport.pdf

Kay, K., & Shipman, C. (2014, May). The confidence gap. *The Atlantic.* https://www.theatlantic.com/magazine/archive/2014/05/the-confidence-gap/359815/

Pipher, M. (1994). *Reviving Ophelia: Saving the selves of adolescent girls.* Riverhead Books.

Vaccaro, A. (2010). Still chilly in 2010: Campus climates for women. *On Campus with Women, 39*(2), 9.

Wiseman, R. (2016). *Queen bees and wannabes: Helping your daughter survive cliques, gossip, boys, and the new realities of girl world* (3rd ed.). Harmony Books.

Biographies

Paige Haber-Curran, PhD, is associate professor and program coordinator for the Student Affairs in Higher Education program at Texas State University.

Grisell Pérez-Carey is assistant director for the Follett Student Leadership Center at the University of Texas Arlington.

Handout 3.1.1

Key Concepts of Gender Socialization

Concept	Description	Examples From Media Sources
Effortless Perfection (Duke University, 2003)	The myth that young women must be academically successful and also demonstrate traditionally female characteristics—such as pretty, thin, nice nails, well-dressed, and nice hair; further, young women are expected to do all of this without visible effort, which is an impossible task.	
Imposter Syndrome (Clance & Imes, 1978)	Self-doubt that involves fear of being found out as a fraud or an imposter, which can stem from the pressure to feel the need to be seen as perfect.	
Ophelia Complex (Pipher, 1994)	A concept in which self-esteem drops for postpubescent girls.	
Crises of Confidence (Kay & Shipman, 2014)	A concept in which girls' and women's confidence declines with experience, which in turn also negatively affects their aspirations to achieve higher management or leadership roles.	
Gendered Leadership Biases	Stereotypes and expectations that exist for individuals based on their gender.	
Queen Bees and Wannabes (Wiseman, 2016)	The "girl code" that operates for young women, which includes the power that cliques play in shaping adolescent girls' lives.	
Chilly Classroom Climate (Vaccaro, 2010)	A concept in which women face environments that are unwelcoming in college classrooms; this involves both overt and subtle actions, such as calling a student "sweetheart" or calling on more men to speak than women. Although outside of a classroom context, similar environments can show up in other contexts for women, such as in the workplace.	

Handout 3.1.2: Examples of Media Platforms and Article Titles

1. Awasthi, T. (2018, April 9). How to give your body confidence a complete overhaul. *Girl With Curves*. https://girlwithcurves.com/give-body-confidence-complete-overhaul

2. Awasthi, T. (2018, July 25). Real talk: It's totally okay to do things at your own pace. *Girl With Curves*. https://girlwithcurves.com/real-talk-its-totally-okay-to-do-things-at-your-own-pace

3. Crampton, S. (2013, May 15). I WANT TO BE HER: SEE. WANT. BE. *Harper & Harley*. http://harperandharley.com/2013/05/i-want-to-be-her/

4. Crampton, S. (2015, March 15). How to deal with negative comments online: 6 steps to responding to negative comments online. *Harper & Harley*. http://harperandharley.com/2015/03/how-to-deal-with-negative-comments-online/

5. Crampton, S. (2018, February 5). My no makeup, makeup look: AKA: My everyday makeup look. *Harper & Harley*. http://harperandharley.com/2018/02/my-no-makeup-makeup-look/

6. Delbyck, C. (2019, January 6). Emily Blunt and John Krasinski look practically perfect on Golden Globes red carpet: Blunt is nominated for her work in *Mary Poppins Returns*. *HuffPost*. https://www.huffpost.com/entry/emily-blunt-john-krasinski-golden-globes-red-carpet_n_5c329f9ae4b0bcb4c25cfbc6

7. Elizabeth, D. (2018, December). Selena Gomez wears "choose empathy" sweatshirt to Pilates class: A message to her haters perhaps? *Teen Vogue*. https://www.teenvogue.com/story/selena-gomez-choose-empathy-sweatshirt-pilates-class

8. Hardy, A. (2018, December). I used to hide my scars with clothing and it changed the way I see fashion: 6 women tell their stories of learning to love their scars. *Teen Vogue*. https://www.teenvogue.com/gallery/women-discuss-how-scars-influence-fashion-style

9. Hardy, A. (2018, December). Why does gender neutral clothing translate to *boys* clothing?: Gucci released a report to see what Gen Z thinks. *Teen Vogue*. https://www.teenvogue.com/story/gucci-chime-for-change-gender-fluidity-clothing-gen-z

10. Hardy, A. (2019, January). Kendall Jenner made this middle school look 2019 chic. *Teen Vogue*. https://www.teenvogue.com/story/kendall-jenner-neon-green-top-balenciaga-earrings

11. Matera, A. (2019, January). Ariana Grande wore pink lipstick and a matching faux fur coat to walk her dog. *Teen Vogue*. https://www.teenvogue.com/story/ariana-grande-walked-dog-myron-pink-lipstick-faux-fur-coat

12. Rearick, L. (2018, December). Shade inclusivity, Photoshop bans, and other major beauty industry wins in 2018. *Teen Vogue*. https://www.teenvogue.com/story/beauty-industry-diversity-moments-2018

13. Royse, A. (2019, January). Is it time to call b.s. on body positivity? *Glamour*. https://www.glamour.com/story/is-it-time-to-call-bs-on-body-positivity

14. Ruffo, J. (2018, December). 8 women on the very real (slightly ridiculous) pressure of the "engagement manicure." *Glamour*. https://sports.yahoo.com/8-women-very-real-slightly-171958663.html

15. Scott, S. (2018, November). Michelle Obama opens up: White House confessions, finding your Barack, living free, an exclusive book excerpt. *Essence Magazine*. https://www.essence.com/news/michelle-obama-essence-cover-december-january/

16. Testino, M. (2018, December). I wore the same red suit for 2 months to make a point about fashion's major problem: Every single choice we make is an act of resistance. *Teen Vogue*. https://www.teenvogue.com/story/marina-testino-fashion-industry-plastic-problem

17. Social Media Hashtags
    a. #NaturalMakeup
    b. #WomenInLeadership

18. Social Media Accounts
    a. Magazine Accounts
    b. E! News
    c. Popsugar

The Mythical Norms of Leadership

Adrian Bitton and Danyelle Reynolds

- Group size: any group size
- Time: Total time is 155 minutes (Part One, 65 minutes; Part Two, 40 minutes; Part Three, 50 minutes)
- Methods: Self-reflection, group conversation, model application
- Materials: Markers, "Who is a leader?" handout, sticky notes, pens/pencils, flip chart paper, commitment cards (optional)
- Multimedia: electronically displaying the Lorde quote on the mythical norm (optional), keeping track of responses (optional)

Overview

In this module, participants reflect on the concept of "mythical norms" in leadership in terms of the social identities, knowledge, traits, experiences, and behaviors that people have been socialized to believe represent effective leadership. Participants will identify points of socialization regarding who can become a leader, and how socialization influences the ways people engage in leadership practice. Finally, participants will investigate the mythical norm and identify ways to interrupt these traditional ideas about leader identity and leadership practice.

Learning Outcomes

- Analyze how a person's lived experience and socialization influences views and assessment of leadership
- Articulate how gender and other social identities get mapped onto leadership
- Evaluate socialization from an intersectional lens

Directions

This module contains three parts that can be facilitated across multiple sessions, or it can be offered during a longer workshop. A break in between the sessions allows for ideas to develop over time, while a more consolidated approach builds a quicker crescendo. Both approaches can be effective; choose which one fits your context.

Part One: Socialization Around Leaders and Leadership (65 minutes)

1. *Overview* (5 minutes). Provide an overview of this session, including the learning outcomes and an outline of how the session will unfold.
2. *Individual Reflection* (5 minutes). Provide each participant with a "Who is a leader?" handout

and a pen/pencil. Ask them to reflect on how they were socialized around leadership and/or who was a leader and write down responses in the top three boxes (top half of the handout).

a. Social Identities: What social identities does this person have?

b. Knowledge: What knowledge and skills does this person possess?

c. Traits: What characteristics and traits does this person embody?

d. Behavior: What does this person do? What behaviors do they practice?

5. *Pair Share* (5 minutes). After participants have had a chance to individually reflect and complete the handout.

6. *Large Group Sharing* (10 minutes). Bring the group back together and ask participants to share some examples from each one of the boxes. Note any similarities and differences.

7. *Cycle of Socialization Review* (10 minutes). Explain that the group will now examine how people are socialized to believe that the characteristics and descriptions that were shared represent society's ideal leader. Visually display or distribute copies of the cycle of socialization (Harro, 2008a). Review the cycle and clarify any components and answer questions.

8. *Personal Reflection* (5 minutes). Instruct the participants to reflect individually upon their own socialization around leadership and who was considered a leader. Direct participants to write answers and thoughts in the three columns on the bottom half of the handout.

9. *Pair Share* (5 minutes). Direct the participants to find a partner (can be new or the same partner as the last activity) and share with one another how they were socialized around leadership and who was considered a leader.

10. *Large Group Report Out* (10 minutes). Bring the large group back together to share a few responses. Record the group's answers to the following questions on a large piece of flip chart paper (one paper for each category: personal leaders, leader identities/characteristics, influences, consequences/shaped experiences):

a. Who did you admire and look up to as a leader (for example: parent, president, superhero)? Why?

b. As a child what messages did you receive about who was (or was not) a leader?

c. What messages did you receive about what leadership is/was?

d. Who or what influenced your beliefs about leadership (for example: family, religious communities, schools, sports)?

e. How were messages enforced or reinforced by what was observed in different spaces (for example: at home, with friends, on TV, at school)?

f. How has this socialization shaped the ways you engage in leadership?

g. Have your thoughts about leaders and leadership changed as you transitioned from high school to college? If so, how?

8. *Closing* (10 minutes). Ask the group to look around at all of the flip chart paper and share what they notice. Are there any trends or points of interest that spark curiosity?

a. Ask the group if these collective flip chart paper lists more or less represent the individual handout they completed.

b. If the answer is yes, ask the group why they believe these lists were similar even though the group comprised people with different identities, backgrounds, and experiences.

Part Two: Mythical Norms and Their Interruption (40 minutes)

1. *Introduction* (5 minutes). Introduce the group to Audre Lorde, the poet, civil rights activist, and scholar. Make sure to name her contributions to society. Frame that this next activity explores her concept of the mythical norm. Ask if anyone knows about this concept. Share this excerpt from her 1984 essay "Age, Race, Class, and Sex: Women Redefining Difference" verbally and visually:

a. "Somewhere, on the edge of consciousness, there is what I call a mythical norm, which each of us within our hearts knows 'that is not me.' . . . . It is with this mythical norm that the trappings of power reside within society" (Lorde, 1984, p. 116).

2. *Small Groups* (10 minutes). Divide the large group into groups of four or five students to discuss the quote. In addition to sharing interpretations and reactions, provide the following questions as a framework for the discussion:

   a. Reflecting on the activities and conversation about socialization, what is the mythical norm of leaders/leadership?

   b. How do your identities align with or oppose those that were identified as the mythical norm?

   c. How has society created a construct around the ideal standards and norms of leaders that we subscribe to even when we do not embody it ourselves?

   d. When did you realize that the mythical norm of leadership was just that—a myth? What experiences or conversations prompted this realization?

3. *Large Group Conversation* (10 minutes). Bring the large group back together to share out some highlights from the small group conversations. Then share the second part of her quote:

   a. "Those of us who stand outside that power often identify one way in which we are different, and we assume that to be the primary cause of all oppression, forgetting other distortions around difference, some of which we ourselves may be practicing" (Lorde, 1984, p. 116).

4. *Return to Small Groups* (10 minutes). Have participants return to their small groups and discuss reactions and these additional questions:

   a. How have you benefited from aligning with the mythical norm of leadership?

   b. How were you sanctioned when you did not align to it?

   c. What is the relationship between intersectionality and the mythical norm of leadership?

   d. How does the mythical norm of leadership reinforce oppression and access to leadership?

5. *Bridge* (5 minutes). Bring the large group back together to share out some highlights

from the small group conversations. Explain that the next activity will focus on the difficult work of disrupting the mythical norm and constructing a new, more inclusive method of socialization around leadership.

Part Three: Reconstructing: How Do We Disrupt This Mythical Norm? (50 minutes)

1. *Introduction* (5 minutes). Remind the group that although there are mythical norms around leadership, they are socially constructed, so we also have the power and agency to change them. This next activity will explore ways to dismantle mythical norms of leadership to make room for others and celebrate the intersecting identities of leaders.

2. *Cycle of Liberation Review* (10 minutes). Ask if anyone is familiar with the cycle of liberation (Harro, 2008b). After a few people share or explain, distribute a copy of the cycle of liberation and review it with the group. Clarify any components and answer any questions.

3. *Pair Share* (10 minutes). Instruct the participants to pair with another participant (preferably someone they have not previously interacted with in any of the small group activities). Have each pair discuss ways and strategies to disrupt the mythical norm of leadership, of how they might move toward (or are moving toward) a liberated sense of leadership. Offer a few tangible examples and a concrete description of what that might look like. For example:

   a. Teachers encouraged all students to cultivate their love of learning and helped them develop their talents in different subjects.

   b. Children were exposed to books and TV shows that represented a wide variety and representation of different social identities and family structures.

   c. People with formal positional leadership positions prioritized developing leadership in younger people.

4. *Large Group Conversation* (10 minutes). Bring the group back together and reference the new flip chart paper hung next to the previous ones from the socialization of leadership and the mythical norm. Facilitate a discussion

in which participants share ideas of what liberation from the mythical norm of leadership might entail. Record responses for each category. Encourage participants to walk around and look more closely at the flip chart papers. Bring the group together and facilitate a discussion using the following questions:

a. Would anyone like to add any new strategies or examples?

b. Which strategies or examples particularly stood out to you?

c. How can we continue to make space for others who embody different identities, skills, traits, and behaviors from those who align with the mythical norm?

5. *Closing* (15 minutes). As you conclude, have each participant make a commitment of how they will disrupt the mythical norms of leadership. Pass out commitment cards and allow participants to record their commitment. When everyone has completed their card, ask the group to form a circle and remind them that commitments are stronger when said aloud. Go around the circle and have each person share and explain their commitment.

Facilitator Notes

Depending on learning style, group dynamics, and environmental constraints, there are multiple ways to adapt this activity to meet learning goals. This may include the use of silent personal reflection time, sticky notes, group share, concentric circle sharing, and more. Facilitators can also spread the three parts of this module across different sessions.

References

Lorde, A. (1984). *Sister outsider: Essays and speeches* (pp. 114–123). Crossing Press.

Harro, B. (2000a). The cycle of socialization. In M. Adams (Ed.), *Readings for diversity and social justice* (pp. 15–21). Routledge.

Harro, B. (2000b). The cycle of liberation. In M. Adams (Ed.), *Readings for diversity and social justice* (pp. 463–469). Routledge.

Biographies

Adrian Bitton is an assistant director of leadership development and community engagement at Northwestern University.

Danyelle Reynolds is the assistant director for student learning and leadership in the Ginsberg Center for Community Service and Learning at the University of Michigan, Ann Arbor.

Handout 3.2.1

Who Is a Leader?

Knowledge	Behavior
What knowledge and skills does this person possess?	What does this person do? What behaviors do they practice?

Social Identities	Traits and Characteristics
What social identities does this person have?	What traits and characteristics does this person embody?

What messages did you receive about who is a leader?	Who or what delivered these messages?	Where and how were these messages reinforced?

Formative Influences Shaping Women's Leadership: Gender Socialization Timeline

Paige Haber-Curran

- Group size: any size
- Time: 75 minutes
- Methods: Presentation of information, individual reflection, small group sharing, large group discussion and debrief
- Materials: Blank sheets of paper and pens (each participant needs one sheet of paper and one pen)

Overview

In this module participants reflect upon their formative years beginning in childhood and create a gender socialization timeline. In this timeline they will identify gendered messages they received and other key influences that played a role in participants' socialization of what it means to have a gender. The module ends with a large group discussion of the implications of these messages in relation to leadership.

Learning Outcomes

- Reflect on one's formative years in connection to gender socialization
- Identify gendered expectations and norms inherent in messages on gender in society

and their influence on one's experiences and development
- Analyze gendered expectations and norms in connection to leadership characteristics, behaviors, and expectations

Directions

1. *Introduction* (5 minutes). Begin by discussing the concept of the social construction of gender, emphasizing that the concept of gender, what it means for something to be feminine or masculine, and what it means to be a woman or man have been created in society and are continuously reinforced. Depending on the experience and knowledge of the group, you may need to differentiate the terms gender and sex.

2. *Large Group Discussion* (10 minutes). Pose this question to the large group: "Where and how do we learn about gender as children?" As you field comments, write the responses on a whiteboard or piece of flip chart paper as a reference point for later in the session. Common responses could relate to family, school, toys, media, faith communities, scouting groups, and so on. Supplement as you see fit. Mention that various factors can

shape the developmental experiences of girls and women—and really individuals of all genders—including social, cultural, political, individual, and organizational systems and dynamics.

3. *Individual Reflection* (15 minutes). Pass out blank sheets of paper to each participant and make sure each participant has a writing utensil. Instruct participants that they will spend the next 15 minutes creating their Gender Socialization Timeline. They should reflect on their formative years, beginning in childhood, and think about what they were socialized to think about gender and how they were socialized to think this way. They should focus on messages they heard about gender, what they felt it meant to be a girl or a boy, how they were taught to behave based on their gender, and anything else that seems salient as they think about gender socialization. Encourage participants to think about the different societal systems mentioned previously (social, cultural, political, individual, and organizational) and to be as specific as they can in their timelines. They can include words, phrases, pictures, and anything else that they find useful. They might also consider how gender socialization messages changed from early childhood into adolescence. Acknowledge that participants have multiple identities, such as race or sexual orientation, that may intersect and connect with their gender identities, and encourage them to think about them as well as they construct their Gender Socialization Timeline.

4. *Small Group Sharing* (15 minutes). Ask participants to form groups of three with people with whom they feel comfortable sharing their timelines. Allow 15 minutes for participants to share salient components of their Gender Socialization Timelines with each other and to identify common themes as well as unique ideas that emerged in the sharing. Ask each group to be prepared to share with the larger group.

5. *Large Group Synthesis* (15 minutes). Bring the group back together for a large group discussion of the Gender Socialization Timeline process. Ask for groups to share common themes

and highlights of small group discussion. Invite students to share how their messages or experiences about gender intersected with other social identities, such as race or sexual orientation. Explain that often gender is approached in society as a dichotomous construct, with "man" and "woman" or "masculine" and "feminine" existing on opposite ends of a spectrum. There are serious limitations to this, as it places individuals in boxes and rewards people who behave according to these expectations and punishes those who do not. It also doesn't acknowledge the wide range of behaviors, expressions, and skills that individuals can and should be able to demonstrate, regardless of gender. Further, approaching gender as dichotomous does not acknowledge the growing number of individuals who do not identify on the gender binary as a man or a woman.

6. *In Closing* (15 minutes). Use the rest of the time to discuss how gendered expectations and messages are experienced today and how they connect to women's leadership. Depending on the group and their experience discussing these concepts, the level of depth in the conversation may vary. Even at a very basic level, identifying gendered messages they received growing up can lead to a great deal of awareness. A number of potential discussion and debrief questions are provided; gauge the level of your group to determine what debrief questions may be most appropriate.

a. In what ways are expectations and messages about gender reinforced in society? On our campus?

b. How do we see these expectations and messages play out in relation to women's leadership—in what ways does it impact how we lead and/or what we expect of women leaders?

c. What structures might exist in our organizations or on our campuses that might reinforce gendered expectations and messages?

d. How might we as individuals be reinforcing these messages and expectations subconsciously?

e. What can we do to combat and challenge these messages and expectations?

Facilitator Notes

It may be helpful for the facilitator to complete the Gender Socialization Timeline activity before the session so you can provide some helpful guidance to the participants who may have questions. Although you are encouraged to share some potential examples with participants to get them started, try to leave the realm of possibilities on which the participants can focus on the activity wide and open so as not to limit what they may include in their timelines.

Biography

Paige Haber-Curran, PhD, is associate professor and program coordinator for the student affairs in higher education program at Texas State University.

Personal Leadership Fairy-Tale Rewrite

Misty Krell

- Group size: 10–25 participants
- Time: 120 minutes; the first two or three activities can be moved to pre-class preparation, as needed.
- Materials: paper or computer for rewriting
- Multimedia: internet connection to view Disney princess fairy tale; Digital Google Book link or printed copy of chapter from Zipes's (1989) *Don't Bet on the Prince: Contemporary Feminist Fairy Tales in North America and England.*

Overview

Through autoethnography (Anderson, 2006) and counter storytelling (Solorzano & Yosso, 2002), students will explore the power of narrative as a tool for reflection and healing. They will rewrite a personal experience in the style of a fairy tale to their childhood self, portraying the type of leader they see themselves as now, or wish to become.

Learning Outcomes

- Analyze how knowledge of our community and ourselves contributes to understanding of our ways of learning about, knowing about, and engaging with our world
- Demonstrate knowledge of social identities and understand how our multiple identities intersect to form complex selves
- Discuss literary and societal trends and representation in contemporary literature

Directions

1. *Introduction and Context Setting* (5 minutes). Many of us grow up reading and rereading fairy tales. These are the first stories we encounter that shape our view of the world and our role within it. Think back to some of your favorite fairy tales; what were the main threads of those stories? Consider who was cast in leadership roles, how gender was portrayed. With which characters did you most relate and why?

2. *Comparing Original Fairy Tales & Feminist Retellings* (15 minutes). For many of us, these stories are faded and tinted in our memory by nostalgia. Childhood fairy tales engage the senses—they are as inherently visual (experienced through pictures and text) as they are auditory (voice modulation of the narrator). Disney has curated several traditional fairy tales online, both illustrated and recorded. Read through Disney's portrayal of the traditional Snow White story on their *Disney Princess* website (n.d.). Compare Disney's version of the Snow White story to the feminist retelling in chapter 6 of *Don't Bet on the Prince*, by Jack Zipes (2014). This is available through Google Books: https://books.google.com/books?id=nOChAwAAQBAJ&lpg=PP1&dq=dont%20bet%20on%20the%20prince&pg=PP1#v=onepage&q=dont%20bet%20on%20the%20prince&f=false.

3. *Group Analysis* (15 minutes). After reading the two stories, engage in large group critical analysis of the Snow White original and *Don't Bet on the Prince*. Questions for conversation:
   a. Notice how characters are portrayed, what is around them, what colors are used.
   b. How are space, privacy, and property utilized or not in the story?
   c. What words and language are used and how do they shape the story?
   d. Who acts, when, and how?
   e. What expectations for each other do characters have?
   f. What takeaways are there for the dominant princess narrative?
   g. What, if any leadership style, is portrayed by characters?
   h. How would when and where stories were written change the story?
   i. How could the background of authors shape the story?
   j. What choices did the author make in the feminist version? What makes it feminist?
   k. Compare analyses from previous questions between the original and retelling.

4. *Creative Rewrite* (25 minutes). The stories we tell ourselves have power. How we cast our roles and those around us in our daily lives shapes our reality. Rewrite a personal experience to your childhood self, in the style of a favorite childhood fairy tale, that portrays the leader you are or wish to become. This personal experience could be a moment of change, clarity, or difficulty. It could be a mundane moment that connected your overall story in unexpected ways. The facilitator should be prepared to offer a concrete example to illustrate this retelling. Dedicate approximately 20 minutes to personal writing. Additional reminders and instructions:
   a. Visually imagine this story as you write it. What do characters look like, sound like, what kind of space do they take? Be intentional around considerations of representation (gender, class, leadership style, sexuality, ability, etc.).
   b. Every story needs a moment of conflict that is resolved; consider how your retelling will approach this.
   c. Question your assumptions; explore where they come from.
   d. Consider what you would like your childhood self to take from this story.
   e. How will you trouble or resolve the dominant princess narrative?

5. *Story Circles* (30 minutes). Divide students into small groups and ask them to tell their stories to each other.

6. *Large Group Debrief* (30 minutes).
   a. What fairy tale and personal experience did you choose to focus on and why?
   b. Did the original fairy tale limit your choices for character goals, decisions, paths? If so how and why? How did you resolve this challenge?
   c. What choices did you make around character representation (gender, class, leadership style, sexuality, ability, etc.)?
   d. How would the telling of this story have been received by your childhood self?
   e. Does this retelling change your perspective of the experience or of your or others' role?
   f. What common themes emerge across stories within the class?
   g. What does all of this tell us about women and leadership?

Facilitator Notes

In retelling their story, students may choose to revisit a personal trauma, or may discover new interpretations of previously unexamined experiences that elicit strong emotional responses, both positive and difficult. Be prepared to pause to allow space for these moments. Because these become collaborative stories when shared, the peers of storytellers will often step forward to support and commiserate during these moments.

Facilitators may choose to assign steps 1 and 2 (or steps 1 through 3) as preparation/homework. In that case, context setting will need to be offered as the assignments are being described.

References

Anderson, L. (2006). Analytic autoethnography. *Journal of Contemporary Ethnography, 35*(4), 373–395.

Disney Princess. (n.d.). *Snow White's story.* https://princess.disney.com/snow-whites-story

Solorzano, D. G., & Yosso, T. J. (2002). Critical race methodology: Counter-storytelling as an analytical framework for educational research. *Qualitative Inquiry, 8*(1), 23–44.

Zipes, J. (1989). Snow White: The Merseyside fairy story collective. In J. Zipes (Ed.), *Don't Bet on the Prince: Contemporary Feminist Fairy Tales in North America and England* (pp. 75–80). Routledge.

Biography

Misty Krell, MAIS, is director of academic and student services for the School of Integrative Studies at George Mason University in Fairfax, Virginia.

Feminine or Feminist Approaches? Leading Across Campus and Community

Modules in this section invite exploration of feminine and feminist approaches to leadership whether the sphere of influence is on campus, the workplace, family, clubs and organizations, or community settings. The activities here are based in deep personal reflection, group discussion, and writing.

Key Ideas

- Role of men in feminist leadership
- Cross-cultural leadership
- Leadership beyond Western cultures
- Praxis
- DS

The Role of Men and Gender-Nonconforming Individuals in Feminist Leadership

Keith E. Edwards

- Group size: any
- Time: At least 30 minutes, but can be extended to allow for more in-depth conversations.
- Materials: No materials are necessary. Participants can be organized in chairs or standing as they are able. Questions/prompts can be displayed on screen or newspaper print. A visible timer can be useful but is not needed.

Overview

This module is designed to help participants think about the complexities of feminist leadership, especially for men and gender-nonconforming individuals. It can be expanded and contracted in terms of the number of questions and the allotted time per question to meet the needs of the participants. The large group conversation using the same prompts used during the questions can extend and deepen the reflections.

Learning Outcomes

- Discuss the benefits of feminist leadership for men and gender-nonconforming individuals

- Describe the challenges of men and gender-nonconforming individuals in feminist leadership
- Identify how they want to engage with feminist leadership consciously given their gender identity

Directions

1. *Preparation.* Set up the room for the concentric circle activity. Options depending on the size of the group and the available space include the following:
   a. Two circles of chairs for all of the participants, with the inner circle facing out and the outer circle facing in.
   b. If space for a circle is not possible, you may set up two lines of chairs facing each other.
   c. If chairs are not available, you may invite the participants to stand if they are able in two circles, with the inner circle facing out and the outer circle facing in.
2. *Introduction* (10 minutes). Provide an introduction to the activity. Include the following talking points, in your own words.
   a. Share a working definition of feminist leadership.

b. Feminist leadership has implications for people of all genders.

c. Gender and sex are not the same thing. Gender and sex are both social constructs. Neither gender nor sex are binary categories even though they are often framed this way in U.S. society. Gender-nonconforming individuals are those who do not conform to society's strict social construction of men or women.

d. We'll be discussing with each other feminist leadership and the impact on, challenges for, and role for men and gender-nonconforming individuals.

e. Share the learning outcomes with the participants.

f. Instruct the participants to form concentric circles as you have arranged (chairs in a circle, chairs in rows, standing, etc.).

3. *Review the Directions* (5 minutes). The facilitators will share questions for discussion. Each pair will have 3 minutes (or another specified time) to discuss each prompt. Then pairs will switch by the outer row rotating clockwise (or your own directions) and participants will discuss the next prompt with a different partner.

4. *Three-Minute Discussions* (20 minutes). Depending on the number in the group, the amount of time, and depth of knowledge and developmental readiness of the group, facilitators should select the best prompts for the group or generate those to best meet the needs of the specific group. The following are offered as possibilities and are not intended to be an all-encompassing list and do not all need to be utilized with each group.

a. What is feminist leadership to you?

b. How might feminist leadership benefit women—individually and collectively?

c. How might feminist leadership benefit gender-nonconforming folks—individually and collectively?

d. How might feminist leadership benefit men—individually and collectively?

e. Should gender-nonconforming folks practice feminist leadership? What might be challenging about this in practice?

f. Should men practice feminist leadership? What might be challenging about this in practice?

g. What harm can be done by men in particular claiming to be feminist leaders?

h. Given your gender identity, how do you want to engage with feminist leadership? Practicing? Supporting? Being accountable to feminist leadership?

i. Given your gender identity, how do you want to support, encourage, or caution people of other genders related to feminist leadership?

5. *Large Group Discussion* (10 minutes). Before concluding the activity, the facilitator will call the group back together for a large group debrief. These short conversations are often just enough to get participants thinking about feminist leadership and the role of men and gender-nonconforming people. Hearing from their partners may affirm their thoughts or challenge them. A large-group conversation following the concentric circle activity is recommended and can be facilitated using the same prompts. Invite participant perspectives and differing perspectives. A short, written self-reflection of 2–3 minutes between the concentric circle activity and the large group conversation may be useful to help individuals collect their own thoughts and perspectives. Here are some possible questions for the transitional individual reflection and/or large group debrief:

a. What are new insights I gained through these conversations?

b. What questions emerged for me about feminism and/or feminist leadership?

c. How might my own exercise of leadership shift as a result of this experience?

Facilitator Notes

1. Please vary the activity depending on the size of the group, the space available, and the prior knowledge and developmental readiness of the group.

2. Different groups may need more explanation about gender-nonconforming individuals than others.

3. Utilize the prompts that make sense for you group. Feel free to make them more specific, such as tailoring it to sorority leadership or in sexual violence prevention student organizations.

4. Facilitator(s) should be ready to engage the participants in the large group discussion. The concentric circles activity is intended to

engage thinking and not be the final product of that thinking.

Biography

Keith E. Edwards, PhD, is a speaker and consultant on sexual violence prevention, men's gender identity, social justice education, and curricular approaches to student learning. He is also a leadership and executive coach.

Cross-Cultural Issues and Opportunities in Leadership

Aoi Yamanaka

- Group size: any
- Time: 60 minutes
- Methods: Self-reflection, presentation, and group discussion
- Materials: Paper and colored pencils or markers

Overview

In this module, participants will begin to develop their own cross-cultural leadership philosophy. The participants will reflect on the ways in which their cultures have influenced their perceptions of leadership, particularly their views regarding gender in leadership.

Learning Outcomes

- Describe our own cultures that are well-recognized as well as those that are not recognized
- Analyze how culture influences one's perceptions of leadership
- Examine how gender influences culture, perceptions of leadership, and leadership

experiences in a community (such as an organization or a college campus)

Directions

1. *Preparation.* Provide the participants with the paper and colored pencils or markers.
2. *Individual Reflection via Art* (15 minutes). Instruct the participants to draw images that represent both familiar and unfamiliar cultures and that express the relationship between those cultures and their perceptions of gender. Be sure to emphasize that cultural influence can be on a small scale (e.g., a value taught by a family member) or on a large scale (e.g., widespread customs or rituals). Ask the participants to include the following in their drawings:
   a. Something that they are familiar with (and that they thus rarely scrutinize).
   b. Something that helps them to navigate the real world but that may not be accurate.
   c. Something that is inherited through socialization and that is influenced by lived experiences.
   d. Something that may not be accurate in unusual or unique situations.
   e. Something that is socially distributed among people with similar social identities but that is not the same for all

of these people (Dugan, 2017; Schütz & Luckmann, 1989).

3. *Large Group* (10 minutes). Invite the participants to explore how what they drew is highly connected to their perceptions of leadership as well as to their leadership experiences in various communities (e.g., an organization, a college campus, a religious group, a workplace).

4. *Small Group Discussion* (20 minutes). Divide participants into trios. Begin by asking the participants to explain their drawings. Then, invite participants to share their reflections on how their cultures have influenced their perceptions of gender and leadership. Possible discussion questions are as follows:

   a. What was it like to engage in this activity?

   b. What did you learn about yourself, your culture, and your leadership?

   c. What surprised you?

   d. How has your culture influenced your understanding of leadership?

   e. How have unfamiliar cultures influenced your perceptions of leadership and your leadership experience?

   f. What common sense assumptions or rules have you been taught regarding gender? How have these assumptions or rules influenced your understanding of leadership, your leadership experiences, and your leadership philosophy?

   g. How do your lived experiences regarding gender relate to your understanding of leadership, your leadership experiences, and your leadership philosophy?

   h. How have you challenged (or how might you challenge) these common sense assumptions or rules (especially those related to gender) so as to emphasize leadership in diverse groups?

5. *Debrief Conversation* (15 minutes). It is important to reinforce the complex influence that one's own culture has on one's leadership of diverse groups. Facilitators should ask the following questions to debrief the participants and conclude the discussion:

   a. What are the implications of what we have discussed for cross-cultural leadership and gender?

   b. Thinking critically, how are your culture's common sense assumptions or rules related to your leadership experiences (e.g., feeling privileged or oppressed because of your gender)?

   c. Given what we have discussed, how will this activity influence your leadership perspectives or practices with regard to leading diverse groups?

Facilitator Notes

1. Facilitators can prepare their own drawing in advance that reflects the first activity. This will help facilitators understand the prompts and provide an opportunity for them to share the drawing during discussions.

2. When instructing the participants during Step 2, make sure to direct them to reflect on gender in their cultures.

3. Instead of instructing the participants to draw conclusions about how their cultures and their leadership relate to gender, instruct them to draw conclusions about how their cultures and their leadership relate to the intersectionality of identities.

References

Dugan, J. P. (2017). *Leadership theory: Cultivating critical perspectives.* Jossey-Bass.

Schütz, A., & Luckmann, T. (1989). *The structures of the life-world* (Vol. 2). Northwestern University Press.

Biography

Aoi Yamanaka, PhD, is a term assistant professor and the associate director of academic services in the School of Integrative Studies at George Mason University.

Gender and Leadership in Non-Western Cultures

Aoi Yamanaka

- Group size: any
- Time: 45–60 minutes
- Methods: Group project, presentation, and group discussion
- Materials: "Gender Equity in Other Countries" handout

Overview

Participants will analyze the relationship between gender-based social justice issues and leadership in cultures on the micro, meso, and macro levels.

Learning Outcomes

- Recognize that Western (or U.S.) perspectives might not be applicable to discussions of social justice and leadership in other countries, especially non-Western ones
- Demonstrate an understanding of the complexity of issues associated with cross-cultural leadership and gender in other countries
- Analyze gender-related social justice issues on the micro, meso, and macro levels

Directions

1. *Small Group Conversation* (20 minutes). Instruct the participants to form groups of three to four people. Provide each group with the "Gender Equity in Other Countries" handout. Instruct each group to examine one gender-related social justice issue in terms of how it affects a country or region outside of the United States.
2. *Reporting Out* (15–20 minutes). Facilitate short group presentations; start by asking each group to share its major findings. Facilitate a discussion using the questions listed on the handout, including the following:
   a. What did you learn? What surprised you?
   b. Why is it essential to analyze other countries' social justice issues from various perspectives?
   c. How is the chosen country or region similar to or different from the United States?
3. *Debrief* (10 minutes). Conclude using the debriefing notes and the following discussion questions. Participants should discuss multiple ways in which Western (or U.S.) perspectives may not be applicable to cross-cultural leadership. As the handout indicates, various factors contribute to gender equity and leadership. Possible debrief questions include:

a. How are other countries' gender-related social justice issues associated with cross-cultural leadership?

b. Why should other countries' social justice issues be a part of your reflection on how best to lead diverse groups?

c. What is your current perspective on cross-cultural leadership? How has it changed?

d. How will you apply what you have learned in this activity to your leadership practices?

e. After completing Activities 1 and 2, describe your cross-cultural leadership philosophy.

f. How would you apply the previous cross-cultural leadership philosophy to your practices when working with people whose cultures or social identities are different from you (such as people from a country where gender equity is not as advanced as it is in the United States, people whose racial identities are different from your identity, etc.)?

Facilitator Notes

Step 1 of this activity could be assigned as a group project in advance. Begin the in-person session with Step 2.

References

Sorrells, K. (2015). *Intercultural communication: Globalization and social justice* (2nd ed.). SAGE.

Biography

Aoi Yamanaka, PhD, is a term assistant professor and the associate director of academic services in the School of Integrative Studies at George Mason University.

Handout 4.3.1: "Gender Equity in Other Countries"

Pick one social justice issue related to gender or leadership; focus on a country or region outside of the United States. What is the issue, and which country or region did you choose?

Why is this an important issue?

Please analyze the issue by answering the following questions. Think about how each of these factors contributes to the issue.

MICRO LEVEL	
Cultural Orientation (e.g., interdependent or independent)	What is the country or region's cultural orientation? Do people there tend to emphasize harmony and limit expression of their own opinions, or do they emphasize individuals' initiative, independence, and opinions?
Communication Style	What communication styles do people in the country or region apply? Are they more direct (e.g., specific and literal) or indirect (with nonverbal cues often provided during communication)?
Facework (e.g., saving one's own face, accommodating others' attempts to save face, or finding ways to help all parties save face)	Do people in the country or region try to save face or try to help others do so? What do they do when they find that others have made mistakes?
Situational Factors	Do any other specific situations contribute to the issue?
MESO LEVEL	
Prejudice, Stereotyping, and Discrimination	Do the people in the country or region engage in gender-based prejudice, stereotyping, or discrimination?
Cultural Groups' Shared Stories and Interpretations	What are some commonsense assumptions or rules that people in the country or region hold? Do any of these assumptions relate to gender?
Religion	How does religion influence the issue?
Power Differences	What power differences exist among people in the country or region?
MACRO LEVEL	
Media	How do the media portray the issue?
Economic and Political Factors	What economic and political factors cause or affect the issue?
Geopolitical Power Influence	How have the country's relationships with other countries caused or affected the issue to occur?

Adapted from Sorrells (2015).

Exercising Feminine and Feminist Leadership: A Storytelling and Echoes Experience

Jennifer M. Pigza

- Group size: Open to any size, as small as four will do
- Time: 60–75 minutes, depending on whether participants already know each other
- Methods: Individual reflection, pairs work, large group discussion
- Materials needed: Several sheets of paper for each person and writing utensils, or instruct participants to bring journals; whiteboard or large paper and markers; a selection of crayons and colored pencils
- Multimedia: You may want to play instrumental music while people are writing

Overview

The exercise of leadership is one of praxis, of both action and reflection in order to transform organizations, ideas, systems, and ourselves. This session creates an opportunity for participants to recall critical moments of their own feminine and/or feminist leadership development, to receive the stories of others, and to compose a reply that draws a thread between themselves and their storytelling partner. This method of storytelling and echoes can be adapted to explore any reflective question and to build community within a group.

Learning Outcomes

- Build understanding of how feminine and feminist leadership are experienced by the self and others
- Engage in meaningful reflection activity that can be replicated in other settings
- Practice listening and meaning-making

Directions

1. *Introductions* (10 minutes). Welcome participants and share a brief purpose for the session: Today we will engage in personal reflection and sharing about how we have experienced feminine or feminist leadership. Next offer time for introductions, even if participants know each other. Choose a one-sentence prompt such as, "My name is ___ and my soul home is ___." Lead the group in three cleansing breaths to allow participants to think about their soul home. Model the introduction and then proceed around the

room. This kind of introduction provides an opportunity for genuine connection without taking too much time and initiates a reflective practice among participants.

2. *Overview* (10 minutes). Explore the meaning of praxis: action and reflection upon the world in order to transform it (Freire, 1994/1970). Invite participants to share how praxis is currently part of their life, education, and leadership. Note these ideas on the board or big paper. Describe how the exercise today of storytelling and echoes is a form of praxis.

3. *Individual Writing* (10–15 minutes). Explain to participants that they will have approximately 10–15 minutes for individual writing and reflection. The focus of their writing will be a critical incident related to their leadership identity. Write the main prompt on the board and pass out paper and pens, as needed. You may want to play music while people write. You may also choose to create a handout with the main prompt and subquestions so that participants can more easily take it home to continue to reflect.

   a. Central prompt: Retell an experience in which you became aware of yourself as exercising leadership from a gendered, feminine, or feminist perspective.

   b. Subquestions: What was the situation? What specifically transpired? Who else was present, and what role did they play in the experience? How did you feel? What did you think? Can you recall smells, tastes, or touches from the experience? What meaning do you make of that leadership experience in relation to your life, education, or leadership trajectory? What calls to be said about the experience?

4. *Pair-Share* (10 minutes). Participants form pairs and take turns reading out loud their stories. After each sharing, the listener can ask a few follow-up questions. If necessary, make one trio; they will need additional time to ensure that all stories are heard.

5. *Individual Work: Composing Echoes* (10 minutes). Invite participants to work independently to craft a response to the narrative that they received. Their echo to the story that

they heard can take three forms. Write them on the board or big paper, or as another handout.

   a. What I think you said: a retelling of the story in your own words

   b. What your story evokes in me: a connective story about my own life that emerged after I listened to you

   c. An interpretive poem or drawing: a symbolic representation or extrapolation of the story that I heard

6. *Pair-Share, Round Two: Sharing Echoes* (10 minutes). Returning to their same pairs/trio, participants now read aloud their responses or describe their drawings with each other. The recipient listens and offers gratitude.

7. *Large Group Debrief* (15 minutes). Engage in a group conversation about the experience of this activity. Possible questions include:

   a. What was it like to write about the focus question?

   b. What was going on for you—emotionally, physically, spiritually, or intellectually—as you engaged in the process of writing and reading your story, listening intently to others, crafting a meaningful echo for your partner, and receiving the echo that was composed for you?

   c. What insights came to you through this experience?

   d. What other questions are you drawn to explore through this method?

   e. What else calls to be said as we finish this session?

8. *Closing* (5 minutes). Thank all participants for their participation. Remind the group that the stories they heard from others should stay in the room; however, individuals can share their own stories, insights, and learnings.

Facilitator Notes

- When describing Step 5, be prepared to share some examples of the echoes. Perhaps engage in a storytelling and echo experience with a colleague or friend as a way to prepare for the session.

- Depending on whether the group is new or established, you may want to explore community agreements for how participants honor what is shared in the room.
- This exercise can be adapted as a personal narrative exploration and echo of any focus question and with any group of people.

Reference

Freire, P. (1994). *Pedagogy of the oppressed* (M. B. Ramos, Trans.; New rev. 20th anniversary ed.). Continuum. (Original work published 1970)

Biography

Jennifer M. Pigza is director of the Catholic Institute for Lasallian Social Action (CILSA) and adjunct assistant professor of leadership at Saint Mary's College of California.

What Difference Does Difference Make? The Effects of Stereotypes, Prejudice, and Discrimination on Representation and Leadership

In this section, What Difference Does Difference Make? The Effects of Stereotypes, Prejudice, and Discrimination on Representation and Leadership, the modules take a deep dive into the current research on gender and leadership traits, behaviors, and effectiveness, as well as on the effects of stereotypes, prejudice, and discrimination on women's underrepresentation in leadership. Students explore the research on wages and promotion, their own implicit bias, and learn 20 terms that reflect the dominant culture's resistance to women's leadership.

Key Ideas

- Race and gender wage gap
- Workplace bias
- Implicit bias
- Resistance to women's leadership

The Gender Wage Gap

Cher Weixia Chen

- Group size: any size
- Time: 80 minutes
- Methods: Analysis and discussion
- Materials:
  - Statistics: http://graphics.wsj.com/gender-pay-gap/
  - Video: http://www.annenbergclassroom.org/page/call-to-act-ledbetter

---

Overview

If trends continue at their current pace, it will take nearly 40 more years to close the gender wage gap (Institute for Women's Policy Research, 2020). The disparities are even greater for women of color. For example, in 2018 African American women earned just 62 cents for every dollar earned by White men, and Latinas are projected not to reach equal pay until 2220 (Institute for Women's Policy Research, 2020). The issue of pay equity is even more pronounced in some parts of the world (Rubery & Koukiadaki, 2016). The gender pay gap ironically is still one major feature of the modern labor market. Scholars have been constantly making efforts to identify the various factors contributing to the gender pay gap and to explore the potential solutions to the gender pay differentials (Gould, Schieder, & Geier 2016). This module is to help students gain a basic understanding of the main proposed causes of and solutions to this issue.

Learning Outcomes

- Practice reading, interpreting, and analyzing the statistics
- Practice analyzing probable causes of the gender wage gap
- Practice proposing potential solutions to decrease the gender wage gap

Directions

1. *Introduction* (10 minutes). Introduce the notion of the gender wage gap in the United States. Provide multiple resources for review.
   a. Ask students to go to http://graphics.wsj.com/gender-pay-gap/. This *Wall Street Journal* website illustrates that women earn less than men in 439 of 446 major U.S. occupations.
   b. Also, according to the National Committee on Pay Equity, African American women earned just 62 cents and Hispanic women earned just 54 cents for every

dollar White men earned, compared to 61 and 53 cents respectively in 2017. Asian American women earned 90 cents and White women 79 cents for every dollar White men earned, compared to 85 and 77 cents respectively in 2017.

c. Students and you can also point their browsers to The National Women's Law Center, which provides a state-by-state analysis called Lifetime Wage Gap Losses for Black Women.

2. *Discussion* (10 minutes).

a. What interpretations can we draw from this material?

b. What about the graphics surprised you most? Why?

c. What might be missing in this data, or not as visible?

d. Would what you learned from the graphics affect your career choice in the future? Why and how?

3. *Review Definitions* (5 minutes).

a. What is the gender pay gap? The difference between men's earnings and women's earnings.

b. What are the concepts of "equal pay" and "pay equity"? Pay equity is considered as a fundamental human right and refers to equal pay between men and women for equal work and work of equal value or comparable worth (Chen, 2011). "Equal pay," as used in the media discourse in the United States, typically refers to "equal pay for equal work or similar work," rather than "equal pay for equal work and work of equal value or comparable worth."

4. *Contributors to the Wage Gap* (10 minutes). Examine the factors that may have contributed to the gender wage gap.

a. Economic factors: the jobs that women do; how jobs are valued; and how jobs are organized.

b. Legal factors: women workers may lack legal protection; the law on equal pay may be inadequate; the access to justice

is limited; the judiciary is not receptive to women workers.

c. Cultural factors: stereotypical ideas about women; the predominant religion within a country may affect the level of women's economic participation in general; colonialism; and patriarchy perpetuated the inferior status of women and affects women's economic participation.

d. Systemic race and sex discrimination is the ultimate and most difficult barrier to close the gender wage gap: job segregation, job evaluation methods undervalue women's work or women's skills.

5. *Potential Solutions* (10 minutes). Explore the potential solutions to the issue of the gender wage gap. For example, in response to the economic factors that may have contributed to the gender wage gap, participants may come up with ideas such as collective bargaining, minimum wage setting, the development of a gender-neutral job evaluation, pay transparency, pay history, job desegregation (such as more women in STEM fields), equal pay audits, and the establishment of a process for remedial settlements of pay equity claims.

6. *Lilly Ledbetter: Video & Response* (35 minutes). Watch the 23-minute video (or this can be assigned in advance): *A Call to Act: Ledbetter v. Goodyear Tire and Rubber Co.*, which is available online: http://www.annenbergclassroom.org/page/call-to-act-ledbetter.

a. Discuss the questions: What did you learn from this video about the causes and solutions of the gender wage gap?

b. Compose a letter to Lilly Ledbetter and share some part(s) of the letter with the group.

Facilitator Notes

When talking about the solutions, students should refer back to the causes first. The video tells the story of Lilly Ledbetter (Ledbetter & Isom, 2013), whose legal battle led to the Lilly Ledbetter Fair Pay Act of 2009. Students are encouraged to explore how women became agents of positive social change.

References

Chen, C. W. (2011). *Compliance and compromise: The jurisprudence of gender pay equity.* Martinus Nijhoff.

Gould, E., Schieder, J., & Geier, K. (2016). *What is the gender pay gap and is it real?* Economic Policy Institute. https://www.epi.org/files/pdf/112962.pdf

Institute for Women's Policy Research. (2020). *Same gap, different year: IWPR says wage gap persists.* https://iwpr.org/media/press-releases/same-gap-different-year-iwpr-says-wage-gap-persists/

Ledbetter, L., & Isom, L. S. (2013). *Grace and grit: My fight for equal pay and fairness at Goodyear and beyond.* Three Rivers Press.

Rubery, J., & Koukiadaki, A. (2016). *Closing the gender pay gap: A review of the issues, policy mechanisms, and international evidence.* International Labor Office.

Biography

Cher Weixia Chen, PhD, is an associate professor in the School of Integrative Studies at George Mason University.

The Workplace Effects of Stereotypes, Prejudice, and Discrimination on Women's Leadership

Graziella Pagliarulo McCarron

- Group size: Open to any size group, but time needed will increase as the group size increases. For a 60-minute activity, a 15–20-person group would work best.
- Time: 60 minutes (please see previous note)
- Methods: Film, quiet self-reflection, small group discussion, large group sharing
- Materials Needed: Easel paper (20 sheets) and markers (20); dry-erase board with dry-erase markers or chalkboard with chalk
- Multimedia: You will need a video screen with speakers or smart room technology with internet access and projection capacity. Load the following film: *How a Simple Experiment Exposed Gender Bias in the Workplace* (Massa, 2017), available at https://toronto.citynews.ca/2017/03/11/simple-experiment-exposed-gender-bias-workplace/.

Overview

In this module, participants explore the effects of stereotypes, prejudice, and discrimination in the workplace (and/or with regard to career aspirations) on women's underrepresentation in leadership. Through a group activity and discussion, participants will explore biases and assumptions, examine personal experiences, and engage in discussion to unpack perspectives on the intentional and unintentional silencing and cloaking of women in professional spaces. Intersectionality will be addressed as a means to highlight the fact that racism, sexism, and other marginalizing "isms" do not happen in singular vacuums and further present barriers to women's leadership. Participants will develop a personal action statement for identifying and combating stereotypes, prejudice, and discrimination in the workplace.

Learning Outcomes

- Relate existing research on the effects of stereotypes, prejudice, and discrimination on women's underrepresentation in leadership to real-world examples
- Reflect on biases and assumptions about the roles of women in the workplace
- Critique current practices in professional spaces (and advocacy approaches) with regard to intersectionality (e.g., sexism, racism, ageism, etc.)

- Develop a personal action statement for identifying and combating stereotypes, prejudice, and discrimination in the workplace—as tool for cultivating women's leadership

Directions

1. *Introduction* (15 minutes). Briefly review the existing research on the effects of stereotypes, prejudice, and discrimination on women's underrepresentation in leadership (for reference, see Owen, 2020, pp. 108–115). Then using the previous summary, introduce the purpose of activity.
2. *Preflection* (5 minutes). Ask participants to do a preflection free-write on the following questions. The facilitator can write questions on the board to help the group with recall.
   a. What do stereotypical, prejudicial, and discriminatory acts against women in the workplace look like today? What examples or biases come to mind? How have things changed or evolved over time? Improved/not improved?
   b. How might this climate change based on industry or context? Examples?
   c. How does this climate support or hinder women's leadership?
3. *Video* (3–5 minutes). Show the video *How a Simple Experiment Exposed Gender Bias in the Workplace* (Massa, 2017).
4. *Group Discussion* (10 minutes). Facilitate a short discussion with the large group relating to the preflection, the film, and the text. The discussion can be guided by the following questions:
   a. What stood out for you in this film?
   b. What emotions emerged for you? Can you share or relate?
   c. Think back to the first question you answered in the preflection. Now think about the film: What challenged you, surprised you, and/or affirmed what you already knew?

   d. Who is missing from the narrative? This question helps participants talk about intersectionality and multiple "isms." For example, does being perceived as "bossy" look differently for a White woman than it does for a woman of color?
   e. How does this connect to what we know about women's leadership? This question leads into the action-oriented part of this module: writing action statements.
5. *Pair-Share & Action Planning* (10 minutes). Ask participants to turn to a partner and discuss their responses and meaning-making of the large conversation. Based on their sharing, each person should come up with a three-point action statement for identifying and combating stereotypes, prejudice, and discrimination in the workplace (as a tool for cultivating women's leadership). Ask pairs to write actions down on easel paper. The facilitator should distribute easel paper and markers to each pair once conversations begin.
6. *Large Group Sharing & Debrief* (15 minutes). Ask each pair to share their personal action statements. As this is happening, the facilitator should use the dry-erase board or chalkboard to jot down common themes. After sharing is complete, the facilitator should summarize the common themes and make relationships back to texts.
7. *After the Session.* The thematized action statements can be compiled and posted online or distributed as paper copies. These will be shared guidelines developed by the learning community that can be enacted by the community.

Facilitator Notes

A core aim of this module is to help the group connect the text presentation of the effects of stereotypes, prejudice, and discrimination in the workplace on women and leadership. The facilitator should ensure that discussions enable participants to critique current societal structures, understand implications, and plan for change agency going forward. Not all participants may share the same views or feel the same urgency and, as such, it is critical to give space to all sentiment while truth-seeking. Prepare to ask questions that begin with the following:

- Can you tell me more . . .
- Can you elaborate for us . . .
- How so?
- Can you help me understand?

Note: It is not within the scope of this activity to discuss implicit or explicit biases in an in-depth manner—particularly since this content is covered in another module. However, participants may touch on bias in the workplace based on history and context and, as such, the facilitator should be prepared to address this topic in the moment or at an alternate time—per the text.

References

Massa, J. (2017, March 11). *How a simple experiment exposed gender bias in the workplace* [Video]. CityNews. https://toronto.citynews.ca/2017/03/11/simple-experiment-exposed-gender-bias-workplace/

Owen, J. E. (2020). *We are the leaders we've been waiting for: Women and leadership development in college.* Stylus.

Biography

Graziella Pagliarulo McCarron, PhD, is an assistant professor of leadership studies at George Mason University.

A Critical Reflection of Gender Bias in Leadership

Leigh Amadi Dunewood, Natasha H. Chapman, and Stephanie Chang

- Group size: any size
- Time: 90 minutes
- Methods: Self-assessment, written reflection (optional), critical reflection, small group dialogue/think-pair-share, large group discussion
- Materials and multimedia: The AAUW Implicit Association Test (IAT) on gender and leadership can be found via a link at https://www.aauw.org/resource/iat/. Project Implicit offers two gender-related IATs (available at https://implicit.harvard.edu/implicit/Study?tid=-1), Gender-Science and Gender-Career, that could be taken in addition to or as an alternative to the AAUW IAT. The following multimedia resources, while optional, may help participants develop a stronger understanding of implicit bias if it has not been introduced previously.
  - Project Implicit (https://implicit.harvard.edu/implicit/)
  - Who Me Biased? (https://www.nytimes.com/video/who-me-biased)
  - Barriers and Bias: The Status of Women in Leadership (https://www.aauw.org/research/barriers-and-bias/)
  - Test Yourself for Hidden Bias: (https://www.tolerance.org/professional-development/test-yourself-for-hidden-bias)

Overview

By encouraging participants to consider leadership as a social construct, this activity will promote a critical and personal examination of gender bias in leadership. Participants will increase their understanding of implicit bias, and explore the ways in which role socialization and implicit biases have influenced their understanding and practice of leadership.

Learning Outcomes

- Explore definitions of implicit bias as it relates to gender expression and identity
- Understand examples of implicit bias as it relates to gender expression and identity in a leadership context
- Examine the role of socialization in upholding Western ideals of leadership
- Identify strategies and resources to help mitigate instances of gender-based implicit bias in leadership capacities

Directions

This module is divided across two sessions and includes participants' engagement in the Implicit Associations Test (IAT). You can choose to engage in the IAT during the first session, or assign it as homework. You might also consider assigning or inviting students' engagement in additional bias assessments between the first and second sessions.

Session One

1. *Introductory Conversation* (10 minutes). In the large group, collect participants' definitions or associations with the terms bias, gender identity, gender expression, and leadership. Provide a brief overview of the AAUW IAT on gender and leadership, which can be found at https://www.aauw.org/resource/iat/, making sure to include a rationale of its purpose and what it is intended to measure.

2. *Complete the IAT* (10–12 minutes). Participants will take the IAT using laptops or tablets. Be prepared to assist those who do not have access to technology and/or to allow this step to be done as homework. Ask participants to make a note of their results (so that they can discuss them in the second session).

3. *Closing* (10 minutes). In the last few minutes, encourage participants to share out a word or brief phrase that describes how they are feeling after having completed the first session.

Session Two

1. *Context Setting* (5 minutes). Provide a quick reminder to participants about the IAT they took in the last session (or as homework), and how it is intended to help them identify their implicit preferences as they relate to women and leadership. While still in the large group, preface that participants may feel unsettled or uncomfortable with discussing their IAT results aloud with others, but that they are encouraged to share to the extent they are comfortable.

2. *Large Group Conversation* (15–20 minutes). To help participants make a connection between bias, their IAT results and their understanding of leadership, pose the following reflection questions:

   a. What prototypes do you have about what a leader should look like and how they should behave?
   b. From what sources did these prototypes originate?
   c. What do you associate with good leadership? Bad leadership?

3. *Small Group Debrief* (15 minutes). Taking the IATs may reveal aspects of self that are surprising and unsettling to the participants. It will be important to assess the developmental readiness of the group as well as their willingness to trust and be vulnerable with one another. Remind participants that revealing their bias should not make them feel ashamed or fearful; rather, it is an important step to name implicit bias in order to work toward mitigating it. Split the participants into small groups where they can discuss any of the following processing questions:

   a. What is something new you learned about yourself after reviewing your IAT results?
   b. To what degree do you resonate with your results? Why?
   c. Choose one word to describe how you are feeling at the end of this small group discussion.

4. Large Group Debrief (15 minutes). After returning to the large group, spend the remainder of time processing the following questions:

   a. How might adherence to specific ideologies/hegemony create in- and out-groups in leadership processes?
   b. In what ways does power influence leadership to reinforce particular understandings of authority? Are there ways in which you may be complicit in this?
   c. How does variation in social identity shape access to leadership development opportunities?
   d. Whose knowledge is centered as valid and essential in the leadership development literature or in other leadership learning spaces?
   e. Are particular approaches to leadership (e.g., assertiveness, empathy, conflict) acceptable based on some social locations but not others?

Facilitator Notes

1. Prior to leading this session, each facilitator should complete the activity and work through the critical reflection themselves. One's willingness to examine, name, and share personal experiences with implicit bias will be a helpful way to model expectations.
2. Variations for using the online IAT:
   a. Use the paper-format Gender-Leader Implicit Association Test found in Northouse's (2018) *Leadership: Theory and Practice*.
   b. Provide a series of verbal prompts for participants to reflect on as described in *Managing Unconscious Bias: Your Workplace Advantage* (Theidermen, 2014) and "Leadership: Changing the Narrative" (Kaya & Chapman, 2020). For example, you may ask the participants to write down the first thought that comes into their head when they imagine "leader." Ask participants to consider the immediate generalities that enter their minds.
   c. Have participants engage in a "Draw a Leader" exercise as shared in "Increasing Metacognitive Capacity Through the Disruption of Implicit Leader Prototypes" (Brooks & Chapman, 2018). Similar to an IAT, an art-based exercise can create dissonance, but may minimize participants' hesitation or resistance to examine it further (Brooks & Chapman, 2018). While an IAT may present cultural bias in its design, the art-based exercise can be beneficial because it is language independent and is not restricted to a list of characteristics (Schyns et al., 2012, p. 14).
3. An additional theory that can be introduced: The cycle of socialization (Harro, 2000) applied to the context of leadership can serve as a useful tool to bring to light the codes of behavior that perpetuate dominant leader prototypes. It can serve as a guide to develop additional prompts to more deeply interrogate our first recollections of leader, the messages we were taught about leadership, the experiences that reinforced or challenged these messages, and how we continue to maintain or disrupt them.

References

Brooks, B., & Chapman, N. (2018). Increasing metacognitive capacity through the disruption of implicit leader prototypes. In J. Dugan (Ed.), *Integrating critical perspectives into leadership development* (New Directions for Student Leadership, No. 159, pp. 53–64).

Harro, B. (2000). The cycle of socialization. In M. Adams, W. J. Blumenfeld, R. Casteñeda, H. W. Hackman, M. L. Peters, & X. Zúñiga (Eds.), *Readings for diversity and social justice: An anthology on racism, anti-Semitism, sexism, heterosexism, ableism, and classism* (pp. 15–21). Routledge.

Kaya, N., & Chapman, N. (2020). Leadership: Changing the narrative. In K. L. Guthrie & D. M. Jenkins (Eds.), *Transforming learning: Instructional and assessment strategies for leadership education* (p. 121). Information Age.

Northouse, P. G. (2018). *Leadership: Theory and practice* (8th ed.). SAGE.

Schyns, B., Tymon, A., Kiefer, T., and Kerschreiter, R. (2012). New ways to leadership development: A picture paints a thousand words. *Management Learning, 44*(1), 11–24.

Theidermen, S. (2014, June 4). *Managing unconscious bias: Your workplace advantage* [Webinar]. In Workplace Matters Series. http://www.workplaceanswers.com/managing-unconscious-bias-webinar-thank-you/

Biographies

Leigh Amadi Dunewood is a graduate student in the student affairs program at the University of Maryland, College Park.

Natasha H. Chapman, PhD, is a lecturer for the global engineering leadership program at the University of Maryland, College Park.

Stephanie Chang, PhD, is the director of student diversity & inclusion in student life at the University of Delaware.

MODULE 5.4

MODULE 5.4

Resistance to Women's Leadership: An Exercise in Terminology

Julie E. Owen

- Group size: Open to any size group. With larger groups (more than 20 people), participants may work in pairs or triads to define terms
- Time: 40–60 minutes depending on the depth and nature of group discussion desired
- Methods: Small group discussion, large group sharing
- Materials needed: Easel paper (20 sheets) and markers (20); OR dry-erase board with dry-erase markers or chalkboard with chalk; copies of terminology, each vocabulary word written on an index card

Overview

In this module, participants explore vocabulary related to the pervasive, cultural, and systemic forces which may affect women in leadership. Through an individual or small group activity followed by a large group discussion, participants will explore how under- or non-representation in the workforce may lead to implicit and explicit constraints on women's advancement.

Learning Outcomes

- Review existing research on the effects of stereotypes, prejudice, and discrimination on women's underrepresentation in leadership
- Develop definitions and examples of terminology and vocabulary essential to describing the implicit and explicit forces that may affect women in leadership
- Reflect on the genderized pressure inherent in leadership and how people's stereotypes about women and leaders can create resistance to women's leadership
- Develop a personal plan for surfacing and naming sexist assumptions in order to create more just and equitable workplaces

Directions

1. *Introduction* (10 minutes). Briefly review the existing research on the effects of stereotypes, prejudice, and discrimination on women's underrepresentation in leadership, as well as the pervasive, cultural, and systemic forces which may affect women in leadership (for reference, see Owen, 2020). Then introduce

the purpose of the activity, which is to familiarize participants with definitions and examples of terminology and vocabulary essential to describing the implicit and explicit forces that may affect women in leadership. Pass out index cards with one vocabulary word selected from the following Terminology List written on each card (do not include the definition on the card). Depending on the number of participants, each person could be given more than one index card/term to define, or with a larger number of participants they can work in pairs or small groups to define terms.

2. *Individual/Small Group Research and Reflection* (10 minutes). Participants are asked to use any available sources (e.g., *We Are the Leaders We've Been Waiting For* [Owen, 2020], internet or Google Scholar searches, etc.) to develop a definition for the word on the card. If they uncover discrepant definitions, they are to pick one that most resonates with their own experiences and understanding. Participants are then asked to think of a real or imagined example of someone facing the form of resistance they are defining. When done, participants should write their definition and example on a whiteboard, or on a sheet of easel paper to post around the room.

3. *Group Presentation and Discussion* (20–40 minutes). Ask each individual or small group to present the vocabulary term they defined, as well as the real or imagined example. After each vocabulary term has been presented, facilitate a short discussion with the large group relating the definitions to the importance of naming and addressing the implicit and explicit forces that may affect women in leadership. The discussion can be guided by the following questions:

   a. What stood out for you in this process?
   b. Which vocabulary terms were you already familiar with, and which were new to you? Are there similar forces that come to

mind that are not included in this list of terminology? Are there definitions posted that you disagree with? How many of these have you experienced? (One variation on this activity is to have students do a gallery walk among all the definitions and check or star those they have personally experienced.)

   c. Which vocabulary terms represent internalized forms of oppression? Which represent overt or explicit forms of sexism? Which represent institutional, cultural, or systemic forces? (One variation on this activity is to have students group the vocabulary terms along these dimensions.)
   d. What can individuals do to surface, address, and counteract these forces?

4. *Pair-Share & Action Planning* (10 minutes). Ask participants to turn to a partner and discuss their responses and meaning-making of the large conversation. Based on their sharing, each person should come up with a personal plan for surfacing and naming sexist assumptions in order to create more just and equitable workplaces.

5. *Large Group Sharing & Debrief* (10 minutes). Ask for volunteers to share their personal action statements. As this is happening, the facilitator might note common themes. After sharing is complete, the facilitator should summarize the common themes and make relationships back to texts.

References

Owen, J. E. (2020). *We are the leaders we've been waiting for: Women and leadership development in college.* Stylus.

Biography

Julie E. Owen, PhD, is an associate professor of leadership studies at George Mason University.

Handout 5.4.1: Terminology List Related to Exploring Different Forms of Resistance to Women's Leadership

Benevolent Sexism. A more understated type of prejudice in which women are stereotyped as affectionate, delicate, and sensitive. Those who hold benevolent sexist beliefs conceptualize women as weak individuals who need to be protected and provided for (Glick & Fiske, 1996). Although these traits and attitudes seem to encompass behaviors that favor women, research has shown that benevolent sexism is just as oppressive as hostile sexism (Glick & Fiske, 2001).

Burnout. Women in leadership, especially those with historically marginalized identities, are vulnerable to burnout. The isolation and constant challenges inherent in navigating traditional leadership environments can exact a large psychological and physical toll.

Colorism/Shadism. Refers to the phenomenon where people with darker skin tones are subject to more prejudice and discrimination. This is illustrated by the "paper bag test" in the late 1800s and early 1900s where people with skin darker than a paper bag were not allowed to work in many establishments.

Confirmation Bias. Because of the ways our brains operate, biases can shape our perception such that we look for information to confirm our previously held beliefs and discount information that contradicts those assumptions.

Discrimination. A biased decision based on prejudice against an individual group characterized by race, class, sexual orientation, age, disability, and so on (Adams et al., 2007).

Double Bind. Occurs when the expectations that women be communal and collaborative clash with the expectations that leaders be agentic. When women encounter people in the workplace, they likely encounter differing sets of expectations about the appropriate balance between communal and agentic attributes. The result of these differing expectations may show up as resistance to women in leadership.

Effortless Perfection. Refers to the pressure people, especially women, feel to be smart, accomplished, fit, beautiful, and popular, all without exerting or displaying visible effort. The effortlessly perfect woman succeeds in all areas (personal, social, academic, career, health, and beauty) and acts as if everything comes easy to them.

Gender Wage Gap. Even when women are represented in various fields, data consistently show a gender wage gap. This gap is typically reported as referring to the median annual pay of all women who are full-time, year-round workers compared to the pay of a similar cohort of men. Recent census data show women earning approximately 81% of what men earn; the median income for women is $41,554, while for men it is $51,640 (U.S. Census Bureau, 2020).

Implicit Bias. Refers to the way people unconsciously and often unwillingly exhibit bias toward others. The Implicit Association Test or IAT (Greenwald et al., 1998) claims to reveal the strength of unconscious associations people make in their minds.

Imposter Syndrome. Refers to a specific form of self-doubt where people fear of being found out as less than worthy or a fraud.

Institutional Betrayal. When schools and administrators fail to take appropriate action, students can experience a phenomenon called institutional betrayal (Linder & Myers, 2018). Institutional betrayal can include failing to prevent abuse, normalizing abusive contexts, creating difficult processes for reporting, failing to adequately respond to instances of harm, supporting cover-ups and misinformation, and punishing victims and whistleblowers (Smith & Freyd, 2014).

Internalized Oppression. Adams et al. (2007) define internalized oppression as the internalizing, or believing, on the part of the target group, the lies and misinformation that the agent group disseminates. They note that internalized oppression is always an involuntary reaction to the experience of oppression.

Miasma Condition. Livers and Caver (2003) define miasma condition as referring to the wariness, defensiveness, and alertness required of those from underrepresented backgrounds in majority workplaces, which taxes one's energy, time, productivity, and creativity.

Microaggressions. The everyday verbal, nonverbal, and environmental slights, snubs, or insults, whether intentional or unintentional, which communicate hostile, derogatory, or negative messages to target persons based solely upon their marginalized group membership. These messages may invalidate the group identity or experiential reality of target persons, demean them on a personal or group level, communicate they are lesser human beings, suggest they do not belong with the majority group, threaten and intimidate, or relegate them to inferior status and treatment (Wing Sue, 2010).

Prejudice. Exerting bias and bigotry based on uniform stereotypes (Adams et al., 2007).

Queen Bee. Refers to a girl or woman who "through a combination of charisma, force, money, looks, will, and social intelligence, reigns supreme over other girls and weakens their friendships with others, thereby strengthening her own power and influence" (Wiseman, 2002, p. 87). Queen bees are often surrounded by sidekicks, pleasers/wannabes, bystanders, targets, and champions.

Racial Battle Fatigue. This term describes the tendency for students of color to constantly worry, have trouble concentrating, become fatigued, and develop headaches when navigating personal and professional spaces that have historically favored White people (Smith et al., 2006).

Stereotype Threat. The apprehension about confirming an unfavorable stereotype about a group to which you belong.

Tokenism. The practice of making only a perfunctory or symbolic effort to be inclusive to members of minority groups, especially by recruiting a small number of people from underrepresented groups in order to give the appearance of racial or sexual equality within a workforce. The result of tokenism is often the appearance of diversity without actual inclusion.

Triple Jeopardy. Women of color in leadership roles may experience triple jeopardy because of the many stereotypes associated with gender, race, and ethnicity that their multiple identities may trigger in others (Sanchez-Hucles & Sanchez, 2007).

References

Adams, M., Blumenfeld, W. J., Castaneda, R., Hackman, H. W., Peters, M. L., & Zúñiga, X. (Eds.). (2013). *Readings for diversity and social justice* (3rd edition). Routledge.

Glick, P., & Fiske, S. T. (1996). The ambivalent sexism inventory: Differentiating hostile and benevolent sexism. *Journal of Personality and Social Psychology*, *70*(3), 491–512. https://doi.org/10.1037/0022-3514.70.3.491

Glick, P., & Fiske, S. T. (2001). An ambivalent alliance: Hostile and benevolent sexism as complementary justifications for gender inequality. *American Psychologist*, *56*(2), 109–118. https://doi.org/10.1037/0003-066X.56.2.109

Greenwald, A. G., McGhee, D. E., & Schwartz, J. L. (1998). Measuring individual differences in implicit cognition: The Implicit Association Test. *Journal of Personality and Social Psychology*, *74*(6), 1464–1180. https://doi.org/10.1037/0022-3514.74.6.1464

Linder, C., & Myers, J. S. (2018). Institutional betrayal as a motivator for campus sexual assault activism. *NASPA Journal About Women in Higher Education*, *11*(1), 1–16. https://doi.org/10.1080/19407882.2017.1385489

Livers, A. B., & Caver, K. A. (2003). *Leading in black and white: Working across the racial divide in corporate America*. Jossey-Bass.

Sanchez-Hucles, J. V., & Sanchez, P. (2007). From margin to center: The voices of diverse feminist leaders. In J. L. Chin, B. Lott, J. K. Rice, and J. Sanchez-Hucles (Eds.), *Women and leadership: Transforming visions and diverse voices* (pp. 211–117). Blackwell Publishing.

Smith, W. A., Yosso, T. J., & Solórzano, D. G. (2006). Challenging racial battle fatigue on historically White campuses: A critical race examination of race-related stress. In C. A. Stanley (Ed.), *Faculty of color teaching in predominantly White colleges and universities* (pp. 299–327). Anker.

Smith, C. P., & Freyd, J. J. (2014). Institutional betrayal. *American Psychologist*, *69*(6), 575–587. http://dx.doi.org/10.1037/a0037564

United States Census Bureau (2020). *Stats for stories: Equal pay day, March 31, 2020*. https://www.census.gov/newsroom/stories/equal-pay-day.html

Wing Sue, D. (2010, October 5). Racial microaggressions in everyday life: Is subtle bias harmless. Psychology Today. https://www.psychologytoday.com/us/blog/microaggressions-in-everyday-life/201010/racial-microaggressions-in-everyday-life

Wiseman, R. (2002). *Queen bees and wannabes: Helping your daughter survive cliques, gossip, boyfriends and other realities of adolescence.* Three Rivers Press.

SECTION SIX

Navigating Organizations and Systems: Metaphors for Women in Leadership

The modules in this section explore the evolution of metaphors for women's leadership journeys, such as concrete walls, glass ceilings, sticky floors, leaky pipelines, and labyrinths. These exercises expose the frequently nonlinear career paths for women through informational interviews with women leaders and personal future visioning. Throughout these modules, students are encouraged to become more wide awake to what provides focus or limitations to their development as a leader and whole person.

Key Ideas

- On-roads, off-ramps (push and pull factors)
- Environmental scanning
- Strategic intelligence
- Dialectical thinking
- Leaning in (or not!)

Applying a Critical Lens: Why Can't Women Just Lean In?

Amy C. Barnes

- Group size: Ideal for a group of 30 or less, but could be adapted for a larger group setting
- Time: 2.5–3 hours
- Methods: Small group discussion and individual reflection
- Materials: paper and markers/pens for groups to take notes
- Multimedia: links to videos (listed throughout the session); laptop and projector.

Overview

Women's leadership literature, including Owen (2020), addresses metaphors like "glass ceilings and sticky floors," highlighted often in workplace culture to motivate women who might encounter oppressive work environments. Supporting women in these spaces is important, and it is imperative that we acknowledge systemic barriers to women in leadership that contribute significantly to their struggle for advancement, recognition, and success. Failure to address these systemic barriers further perpetuates the struggle women face in "climbing the corporate ladder" or competing with men for greater opportunity and leadership positions. The following module invites participants to practice dialectical thinking, to consider the barriers that exist for women's advancement, and to apply a critical lens to the popular book and philosophy, *Lean In: Women, Work, and the Will to Lead* (Sandberg, 2013).

Learning Outcomes

- Understand what dialectical thinking is and why it is important in solving complex problems
- Critique the "lean in" philosophy
- Consider systemic barriers for women in leadership and ways in which the narrative of success can be reconstructed with a more inclusive, critical lens

Directions

This module includes four parts. Depending on your context, you can distribute the parts across several sessions, or offer them in a longer workshop or retreat format. You might also consider translating some of the items, such a video watching, into preparation tasks. This would reduce the amount of in-person time required.

Part One: Introduction to Dialectical Thinking (15 minutes)

1. *Introduction and Example* (5 minutes). Provide students with a definition: Dialectical thinking is the ability to view issues from multiple perspectives and to arrive at a reasonable reconciliation of seemingly contradictory information. Give participants an example: Learning to ski can be both challenging/painful and fun/exhilarating. Some people might choose to argue that you have to view it through one lens or the other. But why can't it be both at the same time?

2. *Brainstorm* (5 minutes). Ask the participants to brainstorm and provide a few of their own examples of dialectical thinking from their own lives.

3. *Explore* (5 minutes). Pose the following question to the group for discussion: How do you feel about reconciling multiple perspectives or truths? Do you feel it is possible for two people with opposing viewpoints to be right at the same time? Why or why not?

Part Two: Apply Dialectical Thinking to Leaning In (50 minutes)

1. *Introduction* (5 minutes). Explain that you will be using dialectical thinking strategies to understand a complex issue—the "lean in" philosophy, by Facebook COO Sheryl Sandberg (2013). Review the importance of listening to others' perspectives, asking thoughtful questions, and approaching controversial topics with dialectical thinking in mind.

2. *Video* (15 minutes). Show the video of Sheryl Sandberg being interviewed for NightLine/ABC News: https://www.youtube.com/watch?v=PuHnC3VJVSA (ABC News, 2013).

3. *Small Group Discussion* (20 minutes). Place the students in small groups and have them explore the following questions. Consider posting these questions on butcher paper/whiteboard or creating a handout to help students recall the questions and to stay focused.

    a. With what aspects of the interview did you agree?

    b. With what parts of the interview did you disagree?

c. Sandberg admits that she views this issue of gender equity in the workplace through her privileged experience and states that she feels a sense of responsibility as a result to help other women. How do you feel her work is helping women? Are there ways in which it might be further limiting women?

d. What is one word to describe your feelings about this discussion and why do you feel that way?

e. How is dialectical thinking playing a role in your conversation or in your own analysis of the video?

4. *Share-Out* (10 minutes). Ask groups to share out a bit of their discussion with the larger group.

    a. How did your discussion progress?

    b. Were there differing points of view in your group?

    c. How did you use dialectical thinking to better understand the issue?

Part Three: Critique of the Lean In Philosophy (45 minutes)

1. *Critique* (10 minutes). Explain the importance of approaching topics like this with a critical lens, especially in conversations where one might be challenging commonly held dominant ideologies (like those that exist around gender and leadership in our society). Share this quote of criticism from bell hooks (2013) and these other resources offering critical perspectives of *Lean In*. Perhaps display this quote via projector.

    a. "Sandberg's definition of feminism begins and ends with the notion that it's all about gender equality within the existing social system. From this perspective, the structures of imperialist white supremacist capitalist patriarchy need not be challenged. . . . Sandberg effectively uses her race and class power and privilege to promote a narrow definition of feminism that obscures and undermines visionary feminist concerns. . . . Her failure to confront the issue of women acquiring wealth allows her to ignore concrete systemic obstacles most women face inside the workforce. And by not confronting the issue of women and wealth, she need not confront the issue of women and poverty. She need not address the ways extreme class differences make it difficult for there to be a common sisterhood based on shared struggle and solidarity" (hooks, 2013).

b. Additional criticism and counterpoints can be found in these articles (links to articles can be found in the reference list):

    i. "Michelle Obama said "sh-t" and people missed her point about the pressure on working women" (Danielle, 2018)

    ii. "'Lean In' Messages and the Illusion of Control" (Fitzsimmons et al., 2018)

    iii. Michelle Obama: "'Lean in' doesn't always work" (CNN Newsroom, 2018).

    iv. "Facebook's Sheryl Sandberg Admits That Parts of 'Lean In' Are Wrong" (CBS News, 2018).

    v. "5 years after Facebook exec Sheryl Sandberg's famous book told women to 'lean in,' it appears that advice may have mixed results" (Cain, 2018)

2. *Small Groups* (25 minutes). Divide participants into small groups to discuss the hooks quote and other critiques that you share. Tell them there will be a large group discussion where each group will be asked to share their thoughts afterward. Put the following questions on a screen or in a place visible to the entire group.

a. How does this quote from bell hooks impact your previous perspective?

b. What part of the quote gave you additional information to consider in your own worldview or perspective?

c. What is the impact of Michelle Obama critiquing the lean in philosophy publicly? When her comment occurred, the news stations focused much more on her use of a curse word than on the content of her comment. Why do you think that happened?

d. How does Sheryl Sandberg's admission that leaning in may not always be the best solution change the conversation?

e. How does this discussion inform your understanding of issues affecting women in leadership? Where will you go from here?

3. *Large Group Debrief* (10 minutes). Have each group provide a short summary of their discussion experience.

a. What is your greatest takeaway from the discussion today about *Lean In*?

b. Did you come into the discussion with one understanding of the concept and leave with any new or different perspectives?

Part Four: Individual Inadequacy vs. Systemic Barriers to Gender Equity in Leadership (50 minutes)

1. *Group Work* (10 minutes). Divide the group into teams (no more than five or six students in a team).

a. Provide half of the teams with the task of brainstorming the category: "Individual inadequacy impacting women's advancement in leadership." This category focuses on individual behavior and what an individual can control or change about their approach or perspective about accessing leadership.

b. Provide the other teams with the task of brainstorming the category: "Systemic barriers to women advancing in leadership." This category focuses on barriers rooted in dominant ideology, hegemony, biases, and social location.

c. Give students 10 minutes to work together in their teams and to brainstorm their list of barriers. Have students write their barriers on a board or large piece of paper that can be posted easily for others to see. Ten minutes will seem like a long time. Encourage them to remember that a good brainstorm will include silence and pauses, but the best ideas often come after the group gets stuck. The following is an initial list that facilitators can use to fill in any gaps for the brainstorm. It is likely that students will come up with more than this if they invest the full 10 minutes.

TABLE 6.1.1 Individual Inadequacy versus Systemic Barriers to Gender Equity in Leadership

Individual Inadequacy	*Systemic Barriers*
Not advocating for yourself	Dominant ideologies about leadership rooted in patriarchy
Underselling your skills and ideas	Maternity leave policies and culture
Not seeking mentors	Disparity of pay
Women focus too much on what is "expected" from others, society, etc.	Underestimating labor division at home (even with a supportive partner)—unequal expectations
Not going after a job because you don't meet 100% of the qualifications	Gender norming starts in childhood—messages we receive from socialization
Women don't ask (for raises, promotions, time, etc.)	Hiring practices—are they truly unbiased?
Worrying about what people will think about you	"Bossy" label and other negative stereotypes of assertive, confident women
Masking the struggle	Patriarchal culture at work
Perfectionism	Sexual harassment
Believing the dominant ideologies about leadership and not seeing emotion, care, and vulnerability as positive leadership skills	Lack of support systems for women at work—especially in a male-dominated environment
Too focused on family needs	Lack of representation of women in leadership roles
Body image keeps us from being visibly up front	Appearance is critiqued and judged
	Difficult to find mentors

2. *Compare and Contrast* (25 minutes). After the students have finished brainstorming, each group presents their list. Compare and contrast the two lists; then, break them into small groups for conversation.
   a. Do you feel that one set of ideas is more significant than the other in hindering women's advancement in leadership and of organizations?
   b. What is the impact of placing the onus on women to overcome the individual or personal barriers on the list? Why is this often the emphasis?
   c. How might a focus on individual inadequacy contribute to hegemony?
   d. What action can be taken to overcome the systemic barriers that exist?
3. *Concluding Thoughts* (15 minutes). To conclude this nearly three-hour experience, invite

a large group discussion. Begin by asking a few people to share what was discussed in the smaller groups. Then explore these questions: We've learned about dialectical thinking, we critiqued *Lean In*, we explored individual inadequacies and systemic barriers. So what? Now what? What will we do with this knowledge and experience?

Facilitator Notes

Possible adaptations to the activities in Part Four, Individual Inadequacy vs. Systemic Barriers to Gender Equity in Leadership, include:

• Assign for homework the creation of the two lists.

- Ask each student to interview three people about these two lists. After they bring their lists to class, they can merge them/rank them to come closer to a Family Feud-like experience (top 100 people say . . .).
- After the lists are made in class, have the students debate which are more impactful to women's advancement (individual barriers or systemic barriers).
- Assign them a side of the debate and ask them to advocate for that side (even if they disagree with it), then debrief the debate by asking about how it felt to defend their side and about what came up in the discussion.

References

ABC News. (2013, March 11). *Sheryl Sandberg: Women must learn to "lean in."* YouTube. https://www.youtube.com/watch?v=PuHnC3VJVSA

Cain, A. (2018, August 6). 5 years after Facebook exec Sheryl Sandberg's famous book told women to "lean in," it appears that advice may have mixed results. *Business Insider.* https://www.businessinsider.com/facebook-sheryl-sandberg-lean-in-problematic-advice-2018-8

CBS News. (2018). *Facebook's Sheryl Sandberg admits parts of "Lean In" are wrong* [Video]. https://www.cbsnews.com/news/facebook-sheryl-sandberg-parts-of-lean-in-are-wrong/

CNN Newsroom. (2018). *Michelle Obama: "Lean in" doesn't always work* [Video]. https://www.cnn.com/videos/politics/2018/12/03/michelle-obama-sheryl-sandberg-lean-in-kate-bennett-sot-nr-vpx.cnn

Danielle, B. (2018). *Michelle Obama said "sh–t" and people missed her point about the pressure on working women* [Video]. Essence. https://www.essence.com/news/michelle-obama-lean-in-book-tour/

Fitzsimmons, G., Kay, A., & Kim, J. Y. (2018, July 30). "Lean in" messages and the illusion of control. *Harvard Business Review.* https://hbr.org/2018/07/lean-in-messages-and-the-illusion-of-control%27Lean_

hooks, b. (2013). *Dig deep. Beyond lean in.* The Feminist Wire. https://thefeministwire.com/2013/10/17973/

Sandberg, C. (2013). *Lean in: Women, work, and the will to lead.* Knopf.

Biography

Amy C. Barnes, EdD, is a clinical assistant professor and director of the doctoral program in the Higher Education and Student Affairs (HESA) program at Ohio State University.

Environmental Scans and Communal Change

Megan J. Hennessey

- Group size: any size
- Time: 60 minutes
- Methods: Business intelligence and strategic development methods
- Materials needed: Handouts 1 and 2 (one copy per person)

Overview

This module explores strategies for successfully navigating the world of work, including finding advocates and allies across the organization, forming coalitions and support systems, and developing multicultural perspectives throughout an organization. By focusing on the strengths and weaknesses of, opportunities for, and threats against the organization, individuals can be united in an actionable communal task that transcends demographic and/or functional barriers. This same way of thinking applies to the formulation of enduring communal relationships that are strengthened by diversity.

Learning Outcomes

- Apply principles of environmental scanning to identify advocates and allies across workplace groups

- Develop a strategic framework for a coalition based on both communal tasks and communal relationships
- Explain the value of multicultural organizational development

Directions

1. *Environmental Scanning* (10 minutes). Distribute copies of "Handout 1: Environmental Scanning." Review the instructions together as a group, and then allow time for participants to complete the SWOT matrix individually.

2. *Four Questions for Individual Responses* (15 minutes). After participants have completed their SWOT matrices, guide them through the following extension of the exercise. Ask the following questions to the entire group, and allow individual time for participants to record their thoughts on their matrices.

   a. Who contributes most to the strengths of your organization? Do these contributions relate mostly to function (e.g., the president contributes to the strength of updated policies and procedures because of the access and resources associated with her role), or to personality-driven behaviors (e.g., the president has a personable and engaging personality)?

b. Who in the organization will benefit from addressing and/or resolving these weaknesses, and why?

c. Who in the organization is best situated to take the fullest advantage of these opportunities? In other words, who can be a bridge between potential opportunities and existing strengths? What makes them so?

d. Who in the organization is best situated to counter these threats or transform them into opportunities? Why?

3. *Group Discussion* (10 minutes). Lead a group discussion about participants' findings from this exercise. Specifically, ask participants to identify if any trends emerged across each area of the SWOT matrix. For example, did they think of the same individual or role multiple times? What are the greatest commonalities and/or differences between the individuals that they identified? How does formal and informal leadership show up in the SWOT matrix?

4. *Building a Coalition* (15 minutes). Now that participants have identified key personnel who contribute to the strengths, weaknesses, and opportunities and who can possibly transform the threats to their organizations, they should begin to plan a coalition of these personnel. Review the instructions on Handout 2 as a group and then allow time for participants to complete the worksheet individually.

5. *Review & Debrief* (15 minutes). Lead a discussion of participants' work from Handout 2. Emphasize that multicultural perspectives strengthen communal relationships. The following questions can be used in a debriefing conversation or in post-session written reflections.

a. The authors of the book *Her Place at the Table: A Woman's Guide to Negotiating Five Key Challenges in Leadership Success* advise that engaging key stakeholders can be done by: (a) working out expectations; (b) securing strategic responsibilities; (c) having key leaders make the case; and (d) seeding storytelling opportunities via strategically placed allies (Kolb et al., 2010, pp. 64–65). Can you think of other ways to engage key stakeholders that are specific to leadership in higher education settings?

b. The ends, ways, and means approach to developing a strategic framework is common in operational planning and further explained in Waters (2011). What are some other frameworks or models we might apply to accomplishing communal tasks and fostering communal relationships across diverse groups?

c. Consider your work on both Handouts 1 and 2. How would the outcomes of your coalition's work change if everyone in the group were demographically homogenous? How would they change if everyone in the group were philosophically/ontologically homogenous?

Facilitator Notes

- Another process for engaging with key stakeholders and negotiating with teams includes: (a) mapping out individuals' priorities; (b) resolving conflicts directly with departments or units; (c) employing a mediator; and/or (d) using data to resolve differences (Brett et al., 2009).

- Critical relationships across barriers are formed by focusing not just on communal tasks, but also on communal relationships. See Kolb et al.'s (2010) work for more information.

- Participants may struggle with differentiating "ways" from "means" on Handout 2. Explain further that the "ways" are actions or processes, while the "means" are resources that facilitate those actions or processes, such as financial support or clear communication methods. The advantage of using this framework is that it drives participants to transcend gender (or other demographic) barriers to accomplishing a shared mission. For example, it is often used in joint military planning processes in diverse teams of various military occupational specialties, backgrounds, and abilities and in uncertain and complex environments.

References

Brett, J., Friedman, R., & Behfar, K. (2009). How to manage your negotiating team. *Harvard Business Review, 87*(9), 105–109. http://search.proquest.com/docview/227821481/

Kolb, D. M., Williams, J., & Frohlinger, C. (2010). *Her place at the table: A woman's guide to negotiating five key challenges in leadership success.* Jossey-Bass.

Waters, D. E. (2011). Understanding strategic thinking and developing strategic thinkers. *Joint Force Quarterly, 63*(4), 113–119. http://search.proquest.com/docview/926433943/

Biography

Megan J. Hennessey, PhD, is the director of the teaching and learning center at Air University.

Handout 6.2.1: Environmental Scanning

Environmental scanning is a systematic process of analyzing your internal and external environments in order to identify strengths, weaknesses, opportunities, and threats (SWOT) of and to your organization. Conduct a brief scan of your own workplace, club, or community organization and complete the SWOT matrix.

STRENGTHS of my organization are:	**WEAKNESSES** of my organization are:
Example: Include areas of expertise and/or excellence, such as transparent communication practices, debt-free financial management, etc.	*Example: Include areas for improvement, such as unclear tenure or promotion policies, lack of diversity, limited leadership development opportunities, etc.*
OPPORTUNITIES that exist for my organization are:	**THREATS** to my organization are:
Example: Include areas of possibility and/or improvement, along with driving forces in the external environment.	*Example: Include areas that are potentially harmful to your goals or mission, such as unstable markets or increased global competition.*

Handout 6.2.2: Ends, Ways, and Means

Considering the ends, ways, and means of accomplishing a task is central to formulating a successful strategic plan. Apply this same methodology to the organizational development of your newly formed coalition by completing the following worksheet. Identify one communal task for the coalition to address based on the SWOT matrix you completed earlier, and then consider how you will form and maintain the communal relationship of the coalition.

	COMMUNAL TASK	**COMMUNAL RELATIONSHIP**
ENDS	*What is the communal task for this coalition? In other words, what specific goal or project will the group work together to accomplish (e.g., diversifying search committee panels institution-wide)?*	*What does enduring success across multiple tasks and challenges look like for this coalition (e.g., a supportive group of employees across all areas of expertise who form a community of practice around the central idea of diversity and inclusion on campus)?*
WAYS	*How will the coalition work together to achieve the end state/goal (e.g., coordinate with the human resources department to clarify and strengthen search committee policies and procedures)?*	*How will the coalition work together to achieve the end state/goal (e.g., plan informal and formal gatherings to discuss emerging issues and plan courses of action)?*

	COMMUNAL TASK	COMMUNAL RELATIONSHIP
MEANS	*What are the methods and/or resources available to the coalition (e.g., representation at the quarterly institutional diversity committee)?*	*What are the methods and/or resources available to the coalition (e.g., the use of mobile discussion tools/apps to encourage frequent and real-time communication on issues)?*

On-Ramps and Off-Ramps: Narratives of Professional Journeys

Graziella Pagliarulo McCarron and Jennifer M. Pigza

- Group size: Any
- Time: 15 minutes for preparation, 45–60 minutes for informal interview homework, and 50 minutes in class
- Methods: Interview, small group discussion
- Materials needed: "On-Ramps and Off-Ramps" handout

Overview

This module explores the notion of on-ramps and off-ramps and push and pull factors (Hewlett, 2007) that affect women, their exercise of leadership, and their career trajectories. The activities take place in two phases: (a) a homework phase that involves the student interviewing a female-identified leader, and (b) an in-class phase in which students compare the narratives they gathered and begin to predict their own. This module gives students an experience in eliciting the narratives of others and then puts those narratives in dialogue with the self.

Learning Outcomes

- Strengthen knowledge of why and how women take career breaks and how individuals and organizations can respond

- Build interviewing and listening skills
- Raise consciousness about the complexities of building flourishing professional and personal lives

Directions

1. *Preparation* (15 minutes). Pass out the "On-Ramps and Off-Ramps" handout. Describe to participants that they will be asked to informally interview a female-identified person about their life and career in relation to on-ramps, off-ramps, and push and pull factors. They should plan to have the questions with them and to take notes during the conversation. Share with students these interview prompts and, perhaps, augment them with your own or group-generated ones.
   a. How would you describe your professional journey?
   b. What factors have helped and hindered you professionally?
   c. What factors have contributed to your choices about life and career?
   d. Have you ever taken a break from your career? What motivated you to do so?
   e. What workplace and personal practices have helped you to stay engaged professionally, or to return after a break?

f. Share the "On-Ramps and Off-Ramps" handout, give them a few minutes to read it, then ask: What on this page resonates with you, surprises you, is missing?

g. What do you wish that 20-year-old you knew about the relationship between career and the rest of life?

h. Is there anything that you shared that you want me to keep confidential? If so, can I share your insights and learnings without sharing the details?

2. *Next Meeting: Large Group Initial Reflection* (10 minutes). When your group next meets, invite students to share their experience of being in conversation with someone about their life and career. This brings the experience of the conversations into the room and reminds them of the topic of the day. Possible initial reflection questions include:

a. What was it like to ask the interview questions?

b. What insights did you gain about being a listener?

c. What did the stories you heard evoke in you?

3. *Small Groups* (15 minutes). Ask students to pull out their "On-Ramps and Off-Ramps" handout (you may need a few extras to distribute). Break participants into small groups of approximately five students each. Ask them to share what they learned in the interview in light of the literature. Invite them to take notes and be willing to share insights and questions.

4. *Large Group Conversation* (15 minutes). Reconvene the participants for a large group conversation.

a. What insights or trends emerged across the informal interviews in your small group?

b. What larger systemic issues might be at play given what you discovered?

c. Whose responsibility is it to respond the issues of on-ramps and off-ramps, push and pull factors?

d. In what ways are gender role expectations changing (or not) and why might it matter?

e. What are the policy or practice implications here?

f. What are the implications for personal action?

Facilitator Notes

Depending on the experience level of the group, you may need to offer guidance about how students should invite someone for an informational interview, how to pose follow-up questions, and how to hold information in confidence (if that is requested). Also, depending on the group, you may want to create an interview guide handout with the questions so that students can take notes while in conversation. Additionally, given the time limits students may face outside of class, it may be helpful to allow students to conduct interviews face-to-face, via phone, and/or via video.

Participants may be surprised by the challenges and real life stories that they hear in their informational conversations. Be prepared to help students hold this complexity while they connect to the literature and larger, global themes about gender and leadership. In the spirit of creating an inclusive space, ensure students that "there is no one right answer" to how career and life is done.

References

Hewlett, S. A. (2007). *Off-ramps and on-ramps: Keeping talented women on the road to success.* Harvard Business School Press.

Biographies

Graziella Pagliarulo McCarron, PhD, is an assistant professor of leadership studies at George Mason University.

Jennifer M. Pigza, PhD, is the director of the Catholic Institute for Lasallian Social Action (CILSA) and adjunct assistant professor of leadership at Saint Mary's College of California.

Handout 6.3.1: On-Ramps & Off-Ramps (Hewlett, 2007)

Reasons for Off-Ramping or Taking Career Break	
Pull Factors	**Push Factors**
• Parenting	• Under-stimulation
• Eldercare	• Lack of opportunity for growth
• Caretaking of non-elder family members	• Work unenjoyable
• Personal health and medical issues	• Work not meaningful
• Retraining and degree completion	• Excessive workload
• Assuming more domestic responsibilities, in general	• Unsupportive work climate (e.g., sexism, racism, or other marginalization)
• Family or partner move	• Dearth of professional role models

Examples of What Organizations Can Do to Minimize Off-Ramping:

- Flex-work arrangements
- Arc-of-career flexibility
- Reimagination of work life
- Continuation of ambition
- Harnessing of activism
- Reduction of stigmas and stereotypes

Examples of What Women Can Do to Minimize the Effects of Off-Ramping:

- Establish and nurture relationships with core colleagues, clients, and contacts
- Consider staying involved in small projects as bridge to on-ramping
- Maintain your presence on professional networks and social media (e.g., LinkedIn)
- Volunteer to keep transferable skills fresh and applicable
- Keep current with industry trends and developments

Examples of On-Ramps
• Professional networking and wise use of social media (e.g., LinkedIn)
• Employment retooling, retraining, and job placement programs
• Temporary, part-time, freelance, apprenticeship, or volunteer opportunities
• Child, family, and eldercare assistance programs
• Entrepreneurship and small business ownership

Hewlett, S. A. (2007). *Off-ramps and on-ramps: Keeping talented women on the road to success.* Harvard Business School Press.

Personal Leadership Labyrinths

Julie E. Owen

- Group size: any size
- Time: 60–75 minutes
- Methods: Individual reflection with drawing and writing; gallery walk; conversation
- Materials: One piece of large paper for each participant; crayons, colored pencils, markers; tape for hanging items for the gallery walk
- Media: Instrumental music to play during individual reflection

Overview

In this exercise, the metaphor of a labyrinth is the entry point for participants to imagine their future selves and then to identify choice points, barriers, and opportunities along that trajectory. After individual reflection and drawing, participants hang their labyrinths around the room for a gallery experience and meaning-making conversation.

Learning Outcomes

- Cast a future vision for themselves
- Identify choice points, barriers, and opportunities to leadership and life, including

predicting on- and off-ramps that might affect one's career trajectory
- Predict possible obstacles, including personal, organizational, and systemic forces that might shape one's journey
- Imagine possible responses to obstacles, both individual and collective

Directions

1. *Welcome* (3 minutes). Welcome participants and describe that this session will invite them to consider their future selves. Not only will we engage in quiet contemplation, we will draw the journey between today and 10 years in the future. How will we evolve across the next 10 years? What are the barriers, opportunities, and choice points along the way? What about those are connected to elements of identity?
2. *Introductions* (7–10 minutes). To help participants enter the room more fully, ask each person to answer a warm-up question. Encourage participants to answer in one sentence. Choose one question, such as: What three words describe how I'm doing today? What went well or was challenging for me this week? The facilitator should also participate.

3. *Imagining the Future* (7 minutes). Invite students to get comfortable either seated or standing (for some, standing allows for better focus). Ask students to imagine themselves 10 years into the future and to create mental images for the following questions. Allow each question to linger so that participants can fully immerse themselves.

   a. Where do you live? What kind of house, condo, apartment, or yurt? Do you rent or own? Where is it located? With whom, if anyone, do you live?

   b. Are you employed? Do you work from home or somewhere else? What kind of job do you have? Is it 9 to 5? Flexible hours? How much money do you make? Do you have health insurance and other benefits? Are you paying off student loans or other debt? For whom are you financially responsible?

   c. Are you partnered? Who is this person? What kind of work, if any, do they do?

   d. What do you do for fun? For renewal?

   e. Who cleans the house? Does the laundry? Takes care of the yard, if you have one? Does the shopping? The cooking and cleaning? Who pays the bills?

   f. Do you have pets? Who feeds, grooms, and exercises them?

   g. Do you have children? How many? When did you welcome them into your family? Did you take time off from work? Were you paid during that time? If you have a partner, did that person take time off from work? Are your children in school or childcare? Who does drop-off and pickup? Are you active in the PTA or other child-focused organizations?

   h. Are you in touch with your or a potential partner's biological family? Have you created a chosen family? How often do you see them? Do they assist you with childcare or other aspects of life? How might they need your assistance?

   i. Now imagine that something goes wrong—you lose a job, a child experiences a critical illness, a family member becomes disabled, a car accident totals your car, and so on—what are your coping strategies?

4. *Crafting Personal Leadership Labyrinths* (20 minutes). With those images in mind, participants will now create a personal leadership labyrinth that shows how they journey from today to that point 10 years into the future. Distribute paper and provide markers, colored pencils, and crayons for optional use. Play music while people create. The labyrinths can take whatever form makes sense to the individual. Prior labyrinths have been spirals, mazes, decision trees, actual trees with branches, street-map directions, and public transit maps. Creativity is to be welcomed. As participants draw their labyrinths, ask them to identify the following:

   a. Choice points or places where they need to make decisions (obtaining more education, seeking a job promotion, relocating, getting married/partnered, becoming a parent, identifying sources of support, working freelance, starting own company or organization, stepping back from work, etc.)

   b. Possible barriers (personal, organizational, systemic)

   c. Possible opportunities (personal, organizational, systemic)

5. *Gallery Walk* (10 minutes). Post the labyrinths around the room and allow time for participants to read about each other's journeys. Ask the following questions:

   a. What similarities or differences do you notice?

   b. What patterns seem to surface?

   c. How do gender, intersectionality, and other elements of identity show up in the labyrinths?

   d. What did you learn about your own leadership labyrinth through the gallery experience?

   e. What questions emerge as you take in the labyrinths?

   f. How does imagining future opportunities and barriers help you develop personal and interpersonal resources such as coping skills, communities of support, and other aspects of resilience?

6. *Closing Conversation* (15 minutes). Invite participants to return to their seats and discuss

the previous questions. In closing, invite participants to take their labyrinths home and to consider saving them for future reflection.

Facilitator Notes

1. In Step 4, the facilitator may choose to offer context for the notion of labyrinths. In this case, the reference point is not a maze in which one can be lost or trapped, but rather a pathway that symbolizes a pilgrimage or journey. While participants may be familiar with images of labyrinths from Roman Catholic cathedrals, like Chartres, labyrinths are evident across many continents and cultures. An internet search of "labyrinth" will yield many images and ideas that can be shared.

2. The leadership labyrinth exercise surfaces choice points, barriers, and opportunities. In debriefing the gallery experience, facilitators can take note of how one person's barrier might be another person's opportunity. For example, the identity characteristics of a White middle-class Christian often yield organizational and systemic opportunities, while the identity characteristics of an immigrant or person of color would likely yield barriers. One question that might emerge: How do we respond to the opportunities we receive through systemic power? What forms of support and other choice points must someone make to overcome barriers and challenge systems?

Note

This module is adapted from the exercise "Draw Your Personal Leadership Labyrinth" in Owen (2020, pp. 139–140).

Reference

Owen, J. E. (2020). *We are the leaders we've been waiting for: Women and leadership development in college.* Stylus.

Biography

Julie E. Owen, PhD, is an associate professor of leadership studies at George Mason University.

SECTION SEVEN

Beware of Precarious Pedestals: De-Gendering Leadership

In these modules, students trouble the notion that women tend to lead in more participatory or democratic styles, whereas men tend toward autocratic or directive styles. Are there really gender differences in leadership? If so, what does it matter? What does the research say? The activities in these modules explore the nature and sources of power, and related concepts such as influence and empowerment. Students will also engage with the theory of culturally relevant leadership learning (Guthrie et al., 2016).

Key Ideas

- Counternarratives
- Culturally relevant leadership learning
- Gendered leadership traits, practices, values

Reference

Guthrie, K. L., Bertrand Jones, T., & Osteen, L. (Eds.). (2016). *Developing culturally relevant leadership learning* (New Directions for Student Leadership, no. 152). Jossey-Bass.

Dominant Narratives and Counternarratives: De-Gendering Leadership

Daniel Tillapaugh

- Group size: any size
- Time: 45 minutes
- Methods: Individual reflection, pair/share discussion, group discussion
- Materials: "De-Gendering Leadership" handout (one per participant), whiteboard or newsprint, markers

Overview

Critical theory often relies on centering the stories and narratives of individuals that are often oppressed by power structures and systems. For instance, critical race theory scholars forwarded the notion of counternarratives, which allowed for the "[n]arratives, testimonies, and storytelling from a minority perspective [to] provide educators with a set of tools to challenge the policies and practices that privilege the experiences and the tacit truths of the dominant group" (Zamudio et al., 2010, p. 5). This is in opposition to dominant or master narratives, which are defined as "the dominant story or taken-for-granted truths" (Zamudio et al., 2010, p. 5). In this exercise, participants will use this notion of dominant narratives and counternarratives to explore ways to de-gender concepts and characteristics of leadership.

Learning Outcomes

- Understand the concept of counternarratives as applied to gender and leadership
- Reflect upon the ways in which students' own conceptualizations of leadership may uphold gender norms and expectations
- Identify new ways of thinking that can create more gender-expansive praxis around leadership concepts and practices

Directions

1. *Introduction* (3 minutes). To begin, ask the group to think of the ways in which concepts of leadership are often gendered within society. A list of these statements should be noted on a board or newsprint.
2. *Large Group Discussion* (5 minutes). After collecting some responses from the participants, the facilitator should provide a brief discussion about the difference between dominant narratives and counternarratives (see Overview of this activity as a starting point). The facilitator might even use some of the statements offered in the starting conversation as a way to demonstrate how some of the statements

may be a dominant narrative (meaning that it upholds dominant ideologies around gender and leadership) and then explore a possible counternarrative to that.

3. *Individual Reflection* (12 minutes). Distribute the "De-Gendering Leadership" handout to all participants and walk the group through the example provided. Provide participants approximately 10 minutes to work independently on coming up with answers to the first two columns (the master narrative and the counternarrative). They should not yet complete the next two columns.

4. *Pair Share* (10 minutes). Ask the participants to chat with a partner seated next to them and share their responses to the first two columns. With their partner, they should discuss their answers to the next two columns collaboratively.

5. *Large Group Synthesis* (15 minutes). At the close of time, come back to the large group. Ask for a few participants to share some of the master narratives and counternarratives they came up with to the large group. Debrief with the group how pervasive master narratives can be around gender and leadership and how that pervasiveness often leads to the marginalization and erasure of some individuals' leadership (i.e., transgender or gender nonconforming students, women in leadership). Encourage participants to reflect on how we all often uphold master narratives in ways that may be dangerous or problematic around leadership and what action steps we can take to be more conscious of understanding the counternarratives that exist. Some additional questions to pose:

a. When you were working on coming up with examples of dominant narratives and counternarratives around gender and leadership, what stood out to you?

b. How are the dominant narratives about gender and leadership perpetuated within society? How do we learn these dominant

narratives and why do you think counternarratives may not be as prominent?

c. Looking back at what you wrote in the far-right column, what are ways in which counternarratives may promote more gender-expansive notions of leadership and de-gender leadership? How might this be useful to us and our larger society?

d. In what ways are the dominant narratives around gender and leadership potentially dangerous or problematic? What can each of us do about these?

Facilitator Notes

Depending upon the group and their familiarity with critical perspectives on gender and leadership, the facilitator may need to provide additional scaffolding around this activity. Participants who have not necessarily examined their privilege or understand the ways in which power, privilege, and oppression are intersected may find this task more difficult. Therefore, the facilitator may need to step in and check in more with certain participants or groups. A variation may be that you have participants work in pairs or trios rather than starting as an individual task. Facilitators may also wish to find some short videos online that also could provide a starting point for discussion on counternarratives and master/dominant narratives.

Reference

Zamudio, M. M., Russell, C., Rios, F. A., & Bridgeman, J. L. (2010). *Critical race theory matters: Education and ideology*. Routledge.

Biography

Daniel Tillapaugh, PhD, is an assistant professor and chair in the Department of Counselor Education at California Lutheran University.

Handout 7.1.1: De-Gendering Leadership Worksheet

Dominant Narratives About Gender & Leadership	*Counternarratives About Gender & Leadership*	*Thinking About the Master Narrative Here, How Might This Be Limiting?*	*Thinking About the Counternarrative Here, How Might This Actually Allow for Gender-Expansive Notions of Leadership?*
Examples Women tend to lead in more participatory or democratic leadership styles because of their emphasis on relationships with others.	Many individuals (of varying genders) practice participatory or democratic leadership styles given their propensity for relationship building and collaboration.	This master narrative reinforces the false binary that women need to be collaborative or relational in their approach and men rarely are.	The idea of using participatory or democratic styles of leadership has little to do with gender and more to do with which style of leadership an individual resonates.

Engaging a Critical Lens on Gender to Enact Change in Leadership

Trisha Teig and Kathy L. Guthrie

- Group size: 10–30 participants
- Time: adaptable, presented here as approximately 2 hours
- Materials: Paper, pens, or materials for students to write; myriad craft materials (paper, markers, stickers, etc.); large poster paper, chalkboard, or whiteboard and markers.
- Variations: Facilitators may utilize this as a brainstorming activity within a larger conversation or create it as a full project with expectation for implementation.

Overview

In this module, participants create a change proposal to disrupt traditionally gendered conceptions of leadership using the culturally relevant leadership learning model (CRLL; Guthrie et al., 2016). Critical application of the CRLL may assist learners in understanding how to reframe historically traditional gendered perspectives of leadership (Haber-Curran & Tillapaugh, 2018) by gaining tools to notice, reflect upon, and work toward ideas and action for change.

Learning Outcomes

- Identify elements of the CRLL model in relation to their own context
- Reflect upon their leader identity in connection to their gender identity and socialization
- Develop ideas to enact change based on reframing gendered issues on campus and/or in their communities

Directions

1. *Introduce CRLL and Learning Objectives* (10 minutes). As a way to ground the participant's experience, the facilitator may need to review the CRLL model (Guthrie et al., 2016). Conclude opening remarks with a review of the module's activities.
2. *CRLL Activity & Reflection Stations* (30–45 minutes). Divide participants into five groups. Each group completes three of the five stations and then the entire group comes back together for collective learning. Each station should be completed in 10–15 minutes, taking 30–45 minutes total. Several stations require smartphones, tablets, or laptops with internet access.

a. *Behavioral Activity: Two Reflections.* Write a brief reflection on how traditional gender socialization may have influenced (or not) your identity as a leader. Write another brief reflection on a time you may have upheld traditional gendered perspectives of leaders or leadership.

b. *Psychological Activity: Creative Expression.* Develop a creative work (poem, drawing, narrative writing) about how you feel/perceive yourself as leader; include to what extent this self-perception is influenced by your gender identity.

c. *Structural Activity.* Research policy regarding gender discrimination on campus. Go outside the classroom to observe structural (building) representations of traditional gendered representations on campus.

d. *Historical Legacy Activity.* Find a media representation (article, photo, video) of the historical legacy of gendering leadership on campus.

e. *Compositional Activity.* Research data for the compositional diversity and representation for leadership positions on campus in relation to gender. How does this compare with comparable institutions?

3. *Debrief & Meaning Making* (20–30 minutes). Following the interactive reflection stations, the facilitator can debrief students' experiences in the various stations and ensure understanding of the concepts included in the CRLL model. Questions may include:

a. What are examples of research each group found for structural, historical legacy, and compositional diversity on our campus?

b. How did you react to reflecting upon your behavior in upholding traditional conceptions of leadership and gender?

c. Would anyone like to share their original work for the psychological dimension?

4. *Change Proposals* (20 minutes). Return participants to their small groups. Instruct them to choose two or three elements of the CRLL model and to use these elements as lenses to address issues of traditionally gendered conceptions of leadership they have observed or experienced on their campus. Students must identify and submit a proposal with one or two ideas to enact change based on reframing/deconstructing this issue on their campus. For example, students might employ the historical legacy lens to propose instituting a campaign for greater representation of women and gender-nonconforming identities in student government executive positions.

5. *Gallery Walk and Debrief* (20 minutes). Following completion of the written proposal, students should summarize their proposals either by writing them on an available board or one large paper. Students can walk around the room to read each other's proposals. Then, debrief the proposals and proposal-making process:

a. What ideas has your group developed about issues/needs on our campus related to gender and leadership?

b. How do these ideas relate back to your understanding of the CRLL model?

c. What aspects of CRLL are addressed by your ideas?

d. How likely are you to present your proposal formally to campus community members, to gather interest for your proposal?

Facilitator Notes

- How the Change Proposal is presented can vary depending on the context and culture of the group (paper, blog, website, poster presentation, traditional presentation, etc.).
- Based on group and facilitator needs, the Change Proposal portion of the module can be a continuation of the current session, homework, or for the following group gathering.

References

Guthrie, K. L., Bertrand Jones, T., & Osteen, L. (Eds.). (2016). *Developing culturally relevant leadership learning* (New Directions for Student Leadership, No. 152). Jossey-Bass.

Haber-Curran, P., & Tillapaugh, D. (2018). Beyond the binary: Advancing socially just leadership through the lens of gender. In K. L. Guthrie & V. S. Chunoo (Eds.), *Changing the narrative: Socially just leadership education* (pp. 77–92). Information Age.

Biographies

Trisha Teig, PhD, is the faculty director of the Colorado Women's College Leadership Scholars Program and a teaching assistant professor for the Pioneer Leadership Program at the University of Denver.

Kathy L. Guthrie, PhD, is an associate professor of higher education, director of the Leadership Learning Research Center, and coordinates the Undergraduate Certificate in Leadership Studies at Florida State University.

Gendered Leadership, Precarious Pedestals, and Beyond

Adrian Bitton and Danyelle Reynolds

- Group size: Open to any size group
- Time: Approximately 2.5 hours in total; sections can be divided across multiple meetings
- Methods: Self-reflection, group conversation and brainstorming, model application
- Materials: Markers, flip chart paper, each peril and description listed on an individual sign, tape, 10 slips of paper for each participant, pens/pencils
- Variations: Consider having participants individually brainstorm a list of traits, characteristics, values, and behaviors commonly associated with leadership prior to the session. Alternatively, have participants identify and bring examples of articles, movie clips, and other multimedia that portray exaggerated tropes of gendered leadership.

Overview

This module highlights traits, characteristics, values, and behaviors associated with leaders. Next the participants will explore how gender gets mapped onto leadership and why it is harmful for all who engage in leadership. Lastly, the group will explore and focus on traits, characteristics, values, and behaviors that promote androgynous styles of leadership.

Learning Outcomes

- Identify traits, characteristics, values, and behaviors commonly associated with leadership.
- Deconstruct how gender gets mapped onto leadership and articulate why it is problematic.
- Revise traits, characteristics, values, and behaviors associated with leadership to construct and promote androgynous leadership styles.

Directions

This module has three parts which can be done in one session or distributed across multiple sessions, depending on your context. Alternatively, some elements can be asynchronous homework. For example, the group work in Part One could be completed prior to the session and then presented and discussed in real time.

Part One: Traits, Characteristics, Values, and Behaviors Associated With Leadership (20–25 minutes)

1. *Overview* (5 minutes). Provide an overview and mapping of this session.
2. *Small Groups* (5–7 minutes). Divide the large group into random but equal small groups. Give each small group a large piece of flip chart paper and markers. Ask the groups to think about people who they considered leaders when they were growing up and then list the qualities and traits of those leaders.
   a. Note: These lists should not be an ideal list of qualities and traits of leaders or how the participants currently describe leadership. Rather, these lists should be a reflection of how participants were socialized around leadership.
   b. Alternatively, ask the groups to reflect upon the explicit and implicit messages of who was considered a leader (in terms of traits and characteristics) or what words were used to describe what leadership was.
3. *Reporting Out* (7–10 minutes). Invite the small groups to come back together and share their lists. Depending on time constraints and number of small groups, invite the small groups to pair with another small group and share their lists. Ask the groups to note similarities and differences between small group lists. Share any additional observations and expand on any traits or characteristics that may need further exploration.

Part Two: Deconstructing How Gender Gets Mapped Onto Leadership (40 minutes)

1. *Introduction & Initial Prompts* (10 minutes). Explicitly state that gender is socially constructed and that there are many ways a person can identify; however, the next part of this activity will refer to gender through the binary of men and women, since that is how many people are first socialized around gender. Pose the following questions:
   a. Can you identify a trait or quality that would stereotypically be associated with women? Have different people share a few examples from the lists.

   b. Can you identify a trait or quality that would stereotypically be associated with men? Have different people share a few examples from the lists.
   c. Was it easy or hard to answer these questions? Remind participants that this exercise shows how gender gets mapped onto traits and characteristics of people (in general) and of leadership.
2. *Gender and Leadership* (10 minutes). Explain that it is often masked by using coded language in leadership. For example, in trait-based theories of leadership (Northouse, 2007) and when describing traits and qualities that are a component of a person's leadership style, the terms agentic and communal traits are often used (Eagly & Carli, 2007; Hoyt, 2007). Examples of agentic qualities are confident, decisive, self-reliant, competent; examples of communal qualities are nurturing, friendliness, concern for others, helpfulness. In behavioral theories of leadership, the language of task-oriented and relationship-oriented behaviors are used (Northouse, 2007).
3. *Small Group Conversation* (10 minutes). Ask the group which set of traits (agentic or communal) are most associated with men and women. Instruct the large group to return to small groups with the lists and code each trait on the list as either agentic or communal by writing an A or C beside it (A for agentic; C for communal).
4. *Debrief* (10 minutes). Bring the small groups back together into a large group and ask the following debriefing questions:
   a. Any observations or reflections about this activity?
   b. Were there more agentic or communal qualities on the small group list? Why might that be the case? Note the overall breakdown among all the small group lists.
   c. How would you describe the process your small group used to code the list? Was it easy to code or more difficult to decide? Why?
   d. Why might gendering traits be limiting when it comes to leadership?

Part Three: Why Is It Limiting to Gender Leadership? (50 minutes)

1. *Discussion* (15 minutes). Facilitate discussion and share theories and trends such as role congruity theory (Eagly & Carli, 2007), imposter syndrome, double bind, effortless perfection (Duke Study, 2003; Owen, 2020), and Harvard's Implicit Association Test for gender and leadership (https://implicit-harvard-edu.proxy.lib.umich.edu/implicit/). This will help the group realize that these experiences or examples are not individual or unique but rather a part of a larger systemic issue that works to reify traditional leadership and gender roles and ultimately prescribes different leadership styles according to a person's gender (within the binary). Please note:
   a. Depending on the dynamics of the group, ask participants to share examples of these trends in their own experiences (or if participants have observed the trends in other groups and spaces).
   b. Make sure the conversation includes overt sexism and misogyny and also benevolent sexism. The group should be able to recognize and articulate why these gendered leadership trends are harmful to all involved in the leadership process, regardless of gender.
   c. Transition into a conversation beyond awareness and into a deeper exploration of the impact of gendered leadership through the lens of the four precarious pedestals (Owen, 2020; Pittinsky et al., 2007).
   d. Clarify that the trends named previously do not reflect every woman's experience in leadership. Similarly, neither do the precarious pedestals. While the precarious pedestals are common trends from narratives and research, they do not represent every outcome possible of women who engage in leadership.
2. *Precarious Pedestals Review* (10 minutes). Explain that the next activity will illuminate some of the differences in the ways that precarious pedestals impact women's leadership experiences. In advance, create four signs for the precarious pedestals, plus one for "other."

Review the signs around the room, and ask if clarification is needed:
   a. Excluding: provides fertile ground for women to be left out of roles and spaces that are seen as traditionally masculine and thus not the right space for women and feminine leadership traits
   b. Misrepresenting: when women are treated as a monolith and then portrayed as inherently different from men
   c. Molding: holding people to gender-based standards that forces women to mold to a feminine style of leadership
   d. Polarizing: only masculine and feminine traits exist as two poles on a line
   e. Other: a catchall of all other answers that might not be represented through the four other signs around the room
3. *Move About the Room* (15 minutes). Explain that a series of questions will be asked. After each question, participants will move to the sign that best represents their personal response to the question. Read each of the following questions. After each question, ask a few participants to share why they chose that particular peril. Review and synthesize responses before moving on to the next question.
   a. Which of these do you observe most often on campus?
   b. Which of these occur most frequently in your classes or academic experiences (group projects, and so forth)?
   c. Which of these do you notice in your student organizations and involvements?
   d. Which of these perils do you think is the most dangerous or harmful to women in leadership?
   e. Which of these impacts your experience the most?
4. *Group Conversation* (10 minutes). Invite the group to return to the seats and facilitate a reflection using the following questions.
   a. How did your answers change throughout the activity?
   b. How do different social identities influence our perceptions or experiences within leadership (e.g., President Obama

and the perception of the angry Black man; Sandra Oh and the perception of the docile Asian American woman)?

c. What are some challenges you might experience if you are working with people who have different conceptualizations of leadership?

5. *Bridge.* Share a concluding thought such as the following: As demonstrated in this activity, there are many different ways in which perils can manifest for women in leadership. In the next activity, the group will work to de-gender leadership and promote more androgynous styles of leadership.

Part Four: Promoting Androgynous Styles of Leadership (40 minutes)

1. *Reminder.* Transition into the next part of the session by reminding the group that it is not only about being able to recognize the harmful effects of gendered leadership but rather that it is a responsibility to actively work to change gendered perceptions of leadership and promote more androgynous styles of leadership.

2. *Individual Work* (10 minutes). For this activity, distribute 10 strips of paper and a pen to each person. Instruct each person to write down 10 qualities, values, and/or behaviors that they feel are most important when engaging in leadership. Share an example: One of the qualities I most value in leaders is transparency. Each person is free to choose any 10. There are no right or wrong answers.

a. When everyone has written 10, tell the group: Although there are 10, five must be eliminated. Crumple five up and throw the slips of paper into the middle of the table.

b. Next instruct the group to get rid of another two so that only three remain. Crumple two up and throw them in the middle of the table.

c. Now eliminate another one so that only two remain.

d. Finally narrow down to one.

3. *Reporting Out* (10 minutes). Go around the room and have each person share the final word/phrase that remains and explain why

it was kept. As each person shares, write the words on a piece of flip chart paper or board so everyone can see the words in a list.

4. *Debrief* (15–20 minutes). Immediately process the activity and the overall collection of activities by asking the following questions:

a. Refer to the list that was just created from the group and ask the group what they notice about the list. Is the list comprised of agentic qualities? Communal qualities? Human qualities?

b. Are any of these qualities inherently feminine or masculine?

c. How would you describe your own leadership style?

d. How have others described you as a leader?

e. Have you ever felt pressure to lead in a certain way? If so, how and/or from whom?

f. Besides gender, how are other social identities mapped onto leadership? And how might these associations affect who identifies as a leader and how a leader's effectiveness can be perceived?

g. What would or could our experience in leadership be like if leadership was de-gendered?

h. What are some action items that we can do to recognize gendered leadership and actively work to de-gender leadership?

5. *Conclusion.* It is important to recognize coded language and false dichotomies when it comes to leadership (not just when it comes to gender, but with all social identities). By raising consciousness around how gender is assigned to leadership and how it affects people's ability to engage in leadership and lead in an authentic way, leadership can become more inclusive of all people and all styles.

Facilitator Notes

This module intentionally features multiple activities to build upon concepts and to scaffold learning. Depending on the participants' level of familiarity with the content, make sure to explicitly name and/or explain leadership trends and theories. This will allow participants to make connections beyond individual experiences or observations and realize the larger system that works to maintain and conceal how gender gets mapped onto leadership. The activities range in group size to allow for more engagement and direct application and demonstration to check for understanding of concepts and allow for peer support in collective learning. Debriefing and making meaning of the activities is very important, so please consider time constraints, group dynamics, demographics, and learning styles in designing and adapting the facilitation.

For additional research and reading about this topic, consult Heilman et al. (2004), Hoyt (2005, 2010), Hoyt and Blascovich (2007), and Rudman and Glick (2001).

References

Duke University. (2003). *Women's initiative: Duke University.* http://universitywomen.stanford.edu/reports/WomensInitiativeReport.pdf

Eagly, A. H., & Carli, L. L. (2007). *Through the labyrinth: The truth about how women become leaders.* Harvard Business School Press.

Heilman, M. E., Wallen, A. S., Fuchs, D., & Tamkins, M. M. (2004). Penalties for success: Reactions to women who succeed at male gender-typed tasks. *Journal of Applied Psychology, 89*(3), 416–427.

Hoyt, C. (2007). Women and leadership. In P.G. Northouse (Ed.), *Leadership: Theory and practice* (4th ed.). SAGE.

Hoyt, C. L. (2005). The role of leadership efficacy and stereotype activation in women's identification with leadership. *Journal of Leadership & Organizational Studies, 11*(4), 2–14.

Hoyt, C. L. (2010). Women, men, and leadership: Exploring the gender gap at the top. *Social and Personality Psychology Compass, 4*(7), 484–498.

Hoyt, C. L., & Blascovich, J. (2007). Leadership efficacy and women leaders' responses to stereotype activation. *Group Processes & Intergroup Relations, 10*(4), 595–616.

Northouse, P. G. (2007). *Leadership: Theory and practice* (4th ed.). SAGE.

Owen, J. E. (2020). *We are the leaders we've been waiting for: Women and leadership development in college.* Stylus.

Pittinsky, T. L., Bacon, L. M., & Welle, B. (2007). The great women theory of leadership? Perils of positive stereotypes and precarious pedestals. In B. Kellerman & D. L. Rhode (Eds.), *Women and leadership: The state of play and strategies for change* (pp. 93–125). Jossey-Bass.

Rudman, L. A., & Glick, P. (2001). Prescriptive gender stereotypes and backlash toward agentic women. *Journal of Social Issues, 57*(4), 743–762.

Biographies

Adrian Bitton is an assistant director of leadership development and community engagement at Northwestern University.

Danyelle Reynolds is the assistant director for student learning and leadership in the Ginsberg Center for Community Service and Learning at the University of Michigan, Ann Arbor.

Personal Narratives of Gender and Leadership: A Modified Fishbowl Conversation

Jennifer M. Pigza

- Group size: no more than 25
- Time: 60–75 minutes, more if the panel is followed by small group conversations
- Methods: panel and discussion
- Materials: a room in which chairs can be arranged in two or three concentric circles, index cards, writing utensils

---

Overview

This module presents an adapted fishbowl conversation that elicits personal narratives of leadership and gender from guest conversationalists and student participants. The session begins with experienced leaders in a facilitated conversation with each other. After this initial conversation, student participants are invited into the circle to ask questions and offer their own insights and experiences.

Learning Outcomes

- Gain exposure to personal experiences of gender, other aspects of identity, and leadership
- Expand confidence in asking questions, being curious, and seeking mentors
- Build a community of support related to leadership development

Directions

1. *Preparation.* Several weeks prior to this session, invite approximately four to six people to participate as panelists in a conversation about their experiences of gender and leadership. Cultivate a diverse panel in terms of experience, place of work, and dimensions of identity such as race, ethnicity, gender, sexual orientation, national origin, and religion. Invite panelists with whom your students will resonate as well as those who may challenge them. Depending on your context and timing, you might enlist students to generate ideas for panelists as well as the initial questions for them. Prepare panelists by sharing the purpose of the session and sharing initial questions, such as the following:

   a. What dimensions of your identity are important to you as you consider your personal exercise of leadership?

   b. What's an experience (positive, negative, neutral) that helped you understand how gender and leadership intersect?

   c. What stereotypes about women and leadership have you noticed and experienced? How do they affect you—help, hinder, frustrate, embolden, something else?

   d. What do you think about the "lean in" framing of women's leadership?

   e. What can your story teach us about gender, identity, and leadership development?

2. *Set Up the Room.* This type of panel is designed to be conversational rather than formal. To encourage intimate engagement, arrange the chairs in the room in a series of concentric circles. The inmost circle should include enough chairs for the panelists, plus two extra chairs. Then, distribute the remaining needed chairs (one per participant) in either one or two concentric circles around the center, depending on the size of the room. Arrange the chairs so that no one's view is blocked. In each of the chairs, place an index card and a writing utensil.

3. *Welcome and Introductions* (10 minutes). As people arrive, direct panelists to the innermost circle and students to fill in the other chairs. Welcome all to the session and remind everyone of the purpose. Explain a few things:

   a. This is not a traditional panel in which each guest will answer all questions in formal turns. The arrangement of the chairs in circles reflects the conversational nature of this gathering.

   b. The facilitator will keep the conversation flowing based on the questions shared in advance; however, panelists are invited to speak freely with one another.

   c. As panelists are talking, participants can use the index card to note questions or ideas you want to explore when we open up the conversation.

   d. We'll begin the conversation with each panelist introducing themselves and then move toward a free-flowing conversation. After about 15 minutes of panelist conversation, students will be invited to take a seat in the panelists' circle to ask questions or offer an observation. Students will enter and exit the panelists' circle for 25–35 minutes and then move to a closing.

4. *Panelist Conversation* (15 minutes). Each panelist will introduce themselves and answer the first question they were sent in advance. From there, the facilitator will help them keep talking, touching on themes of gender and leadership, asking follow-up, and drawing connections.

5. *Student Participation* (25–35 minutes). Invite participants to join the panelists' circle and pose questions or observations. Ideally, multiple students will join the circle across this period of time; the facilitator may need to be encouraging if folks do not volunteer readily.

6. *Debrief and Closing Reflection* (15 minutes). Take a pause after the last remark and thank everyone—panelists and students—for their participation. Facilitate a closing reflection:

   a. Invite a 2-minute silent reflection during which panelists and students can write on their index cards: one personal insight, one curiosity, and one action step that emerged tonight.

   b. Pair-share with a neighbor for about 3 minutes.

   c. Go around the room and invite each person to share one word that captures how they are feeling as you close the session.

Facilitator Notes

The success of this module relies upon the willingness of panelists to share honestly their experiences of gender and leadership and the facilitator's ability to keep the conversation flowing, without a lot of fits and starts. Students respond well to the circular setting because it reduces barriers between them and the panelists. The concentric circle allows for multiple points of eye contact and diffuses (a bit) an expert framework by encouraging all to participate and all to learn.

If time and space allow, this modified fishbowl conversation can be followed by informal mentoring conversations. For example, after the circle conversation closes, invite each panelist to move to a different area of the room for further conversation. Then, ask students to join with them, going to whichever small group is appealing. Drinks and snacks can keep the conversation flowing. This further creates an opportunity for students to connect with each other and for potential mentoring relationships to develop.

Biography

Jennifer M. Pigza, PhD, is the director of the Catholic Institute for Lasallian Social Action (CILSA) and adjunct assistant professor of leadership at Saint Mary's College of California.

SECTION EIGHT

Reimagining Women and Leadership: Strategies, Allies, and Critical Hope

The final section of this text, Reimagining Women and Leadership: Strategies, Allies, and Critical Hope, includes more modules than the preceding sections, because hope combined with strategy is the key to students' long-term leadership development and leadership resilience. The conversations can evolve to address topics such as ally development, how to deal with nonfeminist others, how to avoid activist burnout, and how to maintain critical hope. The modules frequently reference Love's (2013) idea of liberatory consciousness and Harro's (2000) cycle of liberation.

Key Ideas

- Liberatory consciousness
- Cycle of liberation
- Tiny changes
- Social movements
- Forms of civic engagement

References

Harro, B. (2000). The cycle of liberation. In M. Adams, W. J. Blumenfeld, R. Castañeda, H. W. Hackman, M. L. Peters, & X. Zúñiga (Eds.), *Readings for diversity and social justice* (pp. 618–625). Routledge.

Love, B. J. (2013). Developing a liberatory consciousness. In M. Adams, W. J. Blumenfeld, R. Castañeda, H. W. Hackman, M. L. Peters, & X. Zúñiga (Eds.), *Readings for diversity and social justice* (3rd ed., pp. 601–605). Routledge.

Developing a Liberatory Consciousness

Michaela Daystar

- Group size: Open to any size
- Time: 50–60 minutes. Facilitators can reduce the time needed for this activity by assigning the written reflection component (#2 in the Directions) prior to gathering in person
- Methods: Group discussion, self-reflection, partner work
- Materials: Create a handout that lists the four elements of liberatory consciousness and includes the following excerpted quotes. This handout serves as a journal for the session's activities

---

Overview

Participants will explore the four elements to developing a liberatory consciousness (Love, 2013) and the small and large ways in which opportunities to apply these elements show up repeatedly in our daily lives. Participants will identify their learning edges with respect to the four elements of a liberatory consciousness, and practice skills to enact the four elements in daily life.

Learning Outcomes

- Understand the way in which a liberatory consciousness disrupts systems of oppression through everyday awareness and action
- Examine the four elements of a liberatory consciousness in the context of lived examples
- Design and commit to a small action each participant can take to build a liberatory consciousness
- Connect the notion of liberatory consciousness to the exercise of leadership

Directions

1. *Review Concepts* (5 minutes). Review the definition and four elements of liberatory consciousness: Awareness, Analysis, Action, Accountability. Write major concepts on the board or butcher paper.
   a. Emphasize the following:
      All humans now living have internalized the attitudes, understandings, and patterns of thoughts that allow them to function in and collaborate with these systems of oppression, whether they benefit from

them or are placed at a disadvantage by them. (Love, 2013, p. 599)

2. *Individual Reflection & Sharing* (15 minutes). Pass out the handout. Participants take 2–3 minutes for a freewrite reflection about what comes up for them when they consider the four elements. Encourage them to include the feelings that arise for them, to go deeper than their academic understanding of the concepts presented. Then ask them to further reflect for another 1–2 minutes on the following quote, followed by inviting a few members to share their reflection:

The development and practice of a liberatory consciousness is neither mysterious nor difficult, static nor fixed, or something that some people have and others do not. It is to be continually practiced event by event, each time we are faced with a situation in which oppression or internalized oppression is evident. (Love, 2013, p. 600)

3. *Applying the Four Elements, Part 1* (5 minutes). Facilitators can choose one of two options. The choice depends on the level of maturity of participants, and the level of trust and connection within the group.
   a. Option 1: Ask participants to think of one or more situations they have witnessed or experienced that are emblematic of oppression or internalized oppression. Participants should choose everyday examples such as biased comments or jokes, microaggressions, assumptions made about people based on an identity, movies that portray oppressive situations with humor, and so on.
   b. Option 2: Provide several hypothetical examples for participants. The facilitator will need to generate these examples in advance.

4. *Applying the Four Elements, Part 2* (10 minutes). Participants then work in pairs to explore how the four elements could apply. This is a good place to reiterate the importance of maintaining curiosity and nonjudgment. See Facilitator Notes for more insight. For example, if the scenario is that you overhear sexist comments in a workplace setting, the students could ask themselves:

   a. What does awareness mean here?
   b. What analysis can I bring to the situation?
   c. What actions could be taken by different people in this scenario?
   d. What would accountability and allyship look like here?

5. *Making Tiny Changes* (10 minutes). See Facilitator Notes for guidance about tiny changes. After individual reflection, ask students to share in pairs their change commitments. Set up a time in a future session when the pairs will check in about their tiny change experiment. If a future session is not occurring, set up a way for pairs to check in independently.

6. *Debrief* (15–20 minutes). To support participants to thrive inside their vulnerability, lead participants in discussing how they feel about applying the four elements of liberatory consciousness to their lives, and what support they might need to do so. Facilitators can also encourage or assign participants to commit to a small action to put this into practice (described as follows). Consider the following debrief questions:
   a. What becomes possible when we choose to apply the four elements of a liberatory consciousness in our daily lives?
   b. What feelings arise when you consider applying them, and what kind of support might you need in order to do so?
   c. Which of these elements feel the most natural to you, and which feel the most challenging?
   d. Social change is most often the result of numerous small changes and actions made over time by many people. What small action or tiny change can you commit to taking in the next 1–2 weeks to support you in building confidence in the areas that feel challenging?

Facilitator Notes

The central purpose of this activity is for participants to apply the concept of liberatory consciousness to their daily lives. This requires participants to look with curiosity and nonjudgment at situations where socialized oppressive behavior shows up in themselves and others, where greater awareness is needed in order to cultivate a liberatory consciousness. Because many people are socialized not to look at or discuss experiences of oppression and internalized oppression, many of us learn to respond to such discussions with shame and defensiveness. It is therefore important to emphasize the aspect of nonjudgment toward self and others and name any defensive responses that arise in participants. The purpose is not to make themselves or each other wrong, but to strengthen the capacity to be curious, vulnerable, and honest about lived experiences often invisible to us due to the process of socialization discussed in the reading. An excellent resource for building the courage, vulnerability, and curiosity required for this work is Brown's *Dare to Lead* (2018).

The concept and practice of making "tiny changes" comes from the leadership and education organization Shakti Rising (www.shaktirising.org). Tiny changes push against our learning edges; they are powerful life tools for making big personal and collective change, as they shift us in achievable increments in the direction of a much larger vision. It is important, therefore, that participants choose what Shakti calls "tiny changes" that are truly small enough to be achievable, while being relevant to serving the larger vision of developing a liberatory consciousness. Everyone will have a different learning edge and therefore a different definition of "tiny." For some people, talking to a relative about a sexist joke they told would be an achievable commitment on their learning edge. For others, this same action could feel insurmountable, and they would need to work up to it in smaller increments.

Participants may need a bit of coaching to select a tiny change at an appropriate scale for them. Ask them to commit to doing this only once, as the goal here is for them to experience success in pushing their learning edge. You can increase the likelihood for success by having them pair up to check with each other about their tiny changes, and by asking them to share back about the result of their tiny change in a subsequent gathering. For maximum impact, incorporate tiny changes into the structure of the group, having them commit to tiny changes each week that build on

each other, and then review the cumulative impact of those changes after several iterations. Here are examples of tiny changes one could make for each of the four elements:

- Awareness: I commit to one day this week paying attention to the language I and others use, and spending 15 minutes writing in my journal about what I noticed and how I felt about it.
- Analysis: I commit one time this week to having a conversation with a trusted friend or mentor about my values as they relate to an equitable society, and writing these values down.
- Action: I commit to one time this week making a list of actions that address one or more experiences of oppression or internalized oppression. A follow-up commitment could be to take one of the actions on the list.
- Accountability: I commit one time this week to consider what elements of my own "window of understanding" could be helpful in supporting others to increase their own awareness of oppressive systems and behavior. A follow-up commitment could be to seek an opportunity to share this understanding with someone else.

References

Brown, B. (2018). *Dare to lead*. Random House.

Love, B. J. (2013). Developing a liberatory consciousness. In M. Adams, W. J. Blumenfeld, C. Casteñeda, H. H. Hackman, M. L. Peters, & X. Zúñiga (Eds.), *Readings for diversity and social justice* (pp. 599–603). Routledge.

Biography

Michaela Daystar provides leadership and strategic vision coaching and facilitation through her company HeartScapes; she holds an MA in leadership for social justice from Saint Mary's College of California.

Social Change and Inclusive Social Movements: A Case Study

Adrian Bitton and Danyelle Reynolds

- Group size: any group size
- Time: 60–75 minutes
- Methods: Case study, group discussion
- Materials: Case study pieces, pens/pencils, poster paper (optional)
- Variations: Facilitator could potentially have one group read the spotlight article and another group read the letter to the editor simultaneously and answer the same debrief questions

---

Overview

In this module, participants will use a case study to apply concepts of social change, liberation, and inclusive social movements. Participants will explore a campus social change movement and discuss ways to create inclusive social movements.

Learning Outcomes

- Apply concepts of inclusive social movements and leadership practice to a case study
- Identify connections between the case and practices of inclusive social movements

- Apply concepts of inclusive social movements, leadership practice, and reflections from case study exercise to social change movements

Directions

If you do not have 60–75 total minutes for this module, you might consider which aspects can be prework or done online. For example, the reading of the first part of the case study and responding to the discussion questions could be a homework assignment that is then unpacked in real time. Or, Part Two of this module could become a brief research and writing assignment or asynchronous conversation in a course learning system.

Part One: Women in Leadership (45–60 minutes)

1. Have participants read Part One of the case study handout, an article highlighting Oliver & Wells University's first female student government president.
2. After participants have completed reading Part One of the case, separate the group into random but equal small groups and discuss the following discussion questions:
   a. How is Kim's leadership described? Are there any biases in these descriptions? Provide examples.

b. What leadership practices does Kim use to create change on campus?

c. If you were the editor in chief, would you print this article? Why or why not?

3. Allow groups to share some of their responses with the large group. The article holds multiple positive and negative themes, including:

a. How Kim is described by the reporter

b. What methods Kim uses to understand campus and community needs

c. What action Kim takes to create change

d. How Kim views her role in leadership

4. Synthesize group responses, and ask the large group what they think will happen next.

5. Have participants read Part Two of the case study, a letter to the editor from two students working on affordable and inclusive housing policies.

6. In their small groups, have participants discuss the following discussion questions:

a. What stood out to you in the letter to the editor?

b. Does your understanding of Kim's leadership practices change? If so, how?

c. What leadership practices is the student coalition using to create change in the community?

d. What social and personal identity groups are centered in Kim's leadership practice? Which are centered in the coalition's practice?

e. What suggestions could be helpful in connecting Kim to the wider student body she represents?

f. If you were the editor in chief, would you print this letter to the editor? Why or why not?

7. Allow groups to share some of their responses with the large group.

8. Explain to learners that, while this is a fictional case, this example highlights some of the realities of social movement and creating sustainable change. These can include, but are not limited to, tending to power dynamics,

understanding community context, building inclusive movements, and taking collaborative steps toward action.

9. Transition into a conversation of applying the concepts from the case to actual social movements.

Part Two: Applying Concepts to Social Movements (15–30 minutes)

1. Explain that learners are going to connect the lessons learned in the first part of the module to real social movements. Choose one movement about which learners will have working knowledge. This could be a change movement on campus, in the institution's local community, or a larger societal change movement. Invest a few minutes reviewing the basics of the social movement that you have chosen for this part of the module.

2. Have participants discuss the following debrief questions:

a. What levers/methods of change are prioritized or privileged in social change work?

b. How is women's liberation tied to other social movements?

c. Think about other social movements that have been deemed "successful"—what aspects/elements/strategies contributed to their success?

d. How does liberation connect to the concept of intersectionality?

Biographies

Adrian Bitton is an assistant director of leadership development and community engagement at Northwestern University.

Danyelle Reynolds is the assistant director for student learning and leadership in the Ginsberg Center for Community Service and Learning at the University of Michigan, Ann Arbor.

Handout 8.2.1: Case Study: Creating a Campus Movement

Characters
- *Tracey Davis:* A writer for the Oliver & Wells daily student newspaper, *The Daily Oak*.
- *Kim Park:* The newly elected student government president. Has been involved in student government for the past 2 years, and is excited to bring about change on campus.
- *Alex Baron and Ari Bond:* Students from a student coalition on campus.
- *Vice President Edwards:* The vice president for student affairs at Oliver & Wells University. Has been at Oliver & Wells for 15 years, and has worked with the past 14 student government administrations.
- *President Clark:* The president of Oliver & Wells University. Has been in this role for the past 3 years and works to cultivate a reputation of excellence for the university.

Setting
Oliver & Wells is a mid-sized university in the Midwest region. Located in a suburban region, it is 20 miles outside of a major city. Next year, the university will be celebrating its 175-year anniversary with students and its strong alumni base. In the last 10 years, the university has focused on three major priorities: providing more internship and job opportunities for students, developing strong relationships with local business leaders, and supporting a diverse body of students, faculty, and staff.

Part One: News Article

SIX MONTHS IN: FIRST FEMALE STUDENT GOVERNMENT PRESIDENT IN 50 YEARS WORKS TO CREATE CHANGE

Tracey Davis, Campus news reporter

Six months into her role as student government president, Kim Park has made a name for herself. During the election last semester, her ENGAGE campaign's work to increase student voter turnout in the student government election led to the largest turnout in a decade. In her time in office, Park has gained a reputation for being tough as nails, but also a caring and nurturing campus leader. I had the pleasure of meeting with Park to talk about her plans for the upcoming year and what her momentous election represents for her and the student body.

Park walks into our meeting with her head held high, wearing a stylish dress suit and pin that match the school's colors. With an air of confidence, I'm surprised when she greets me familiarly by name and says, "Call me Kim."

TD: Although your ENGAGE campaign ran on a platform of better student input on the student activity fee students pay each semester, your administration has been tackling a lot of campus issues—parking, a student food pantry, affordable housing. Which of these initiatives are you most excited about?

KP: I'm most excited about advocating for more affordable housing on campus and the surrounding Forest Glen community. During the campaign, and in my weekly open coffee hours in the Main Learning Center, people talk about how expensive housing is. Students just can't afford to live in this area, and no previous student government administration has addressed this problem. I want to ensure every hardworking student has an affordable place to live while pursuing their education.

TD: What are some of the things you're most proud of, six months into this role?

KP: In this journey, I'm really proud of our ability to get work done for students. We've made it a priority to go to different schools and colleges, different student orgs, and listen to what people need. Because of that, the carpool parking pass we worked with the Parking Department to develop has saved hundreds of dollars for students driving to and around campus. The student food pantry helps eliminate food waste and provides quality food to people who can't afford it. And we've started some good conversations with campus leaders about affordable housing.

TD: What can you tell us about these conversations?

KP: Well, some of them have been with students. Last semester, we did a town hall with Greek leaders across campus. We thought that since Greek students make up 35% of the student population, this would be a good group to start with. We also sat down with the director of university housing and a couple of landlords. Finally, I've been able to solidify a monthly joint meeting with Vice President Edwards and President Clark to talk about the state of the campus. We continue to talk about the lack of affordable housing, and they're interested in addressing it.

TD: How can people get more involved?

KP: If people want to learn more, the student government housing affordability task force meets on Tuesdays at the Cafe. They can also email the committee at housingaffordability@oliverwells.edu.

TD: Any last words?

KP: As a feminist and a leader, I work hard to be a voice for the voiceless on campus. I care about creating spaces in which women on campus can be safe, heard, and valued. As a team, we amplify the voices of so many on campus, and challenge the status quo. I want to continue that momentum to make this campus the best it can be.

Part Two: Letter to the Editor

LETTER TO THE EDITOR: WHERE'S KIM PARK?

We are writing in response to last week's article spotlighting the student government president, Kim Park.

Though Park said she wants to be a voice for the voiceless, she did not consider those of us who have a voice and have been silenced by the structure of this university. We represent the Coalition for Inclusive Housing, and have been advocating for affordable and inclusive housing options on and off campus for over two years. This coalition represents about 60 student organizations, over 50% of the student organizations on this campus.

In the last two years, we have compiled information about the difficulties students have had around housing in our community. While affordability is an issue, we've also learned that there are practices making it hard for other students to find housing. Multiple students have claimed employees of ACME Housing have "lost" the rental applications of students of color. Students who are gender nonconforming and trans* continue to name their frustrations with landlords and property owners in the area. Students with physical disabilities struggle to find housing that is physically accessible. Additionally, one of the most egregious rental property management companies is owned by a member of the university's board of governors. All of this information was shared with Park and her team during the campaign season, but no one has followed up with us after the election.

In the last year, our coalition has been working with students and Forest Glen community leaders to create a citywide ordinance outlining standards for housing, including a nondiscrimination policy and the creation of a renters' union that will benefit all members of our community.

We are glad that the administration has been meeting with Park. We have had a hard time getting information from the director of housing, and meetings with Vice President Edwards and President Clark have been rescheduled five times in the last year. It seems the administration is willing to talk to some students about issues that concern them, but not all. We wonder—has Park brought up the fact that students don't have access to the university administration? Or that a member of the board of governors would immediately be in violation of the housing ordinance if it passes?

We recognize that the voice of a student government president holds more power than ours right now. And we recognize that there has been sufficient work happening in student government this year. But we also want the work that has been happening in this coalition to be built upon, not recreated by a committee.

Alex Baron, history and sociology
Ari Bond, mechanical engineering

Leadership Action Plan: Committing to the Struggle and Sustaining Critical Hope

Maritza Torres and Erica Wiborg

- Group size: Any group size
- Time: 75 Minutes
- Methods used: Reflection, pair/share, dialogue
- Materials needed: Blank sheets of paper for journaling, printed Handout, pens/pencils

Overview

Participants will create a leadership action plan grounded in Love's (2013) idea of liberatory consciousness and Harro's (2000) cycle of liberation. This activity encourages participants to reflect critically on experiences and incidents of injustices that resonate with their identities, values, and beliefs. The purpose of this activity is to have participants create a tangible action plan that will aid in the maintenance of critical hope and in their capacity for creating change.

Learning Outcomes

- Analyze a personal situation they perceived to be unjust in a specific context (for example a community, organization, or group they care about)

- Discern possible actions for liberatory consciousness and critical hope in order to change systems of oppression
- Relate these actions to other possible contexts and their own leadership development

Directions

1. *Introduction* (2 minutes). Use the overview and learning outcomes as a reference point.
2. *Journal Jumpstart* (15 minutes). Share with the participants that prior to developing their action plan, they will begin with a timed, pen-to-paper reflection. This means they will write on each prompt until the time is up. Distribute the blank sheets of paper and pens to the participants, and have them respond to the following prompts. You might consider posting/writing the comments on the walls to help participants focus.
   a. Think of a leadership situation where you sensed something was unjust or wrong, a time when you worked with others and something occurred that felt unfair, icky, or wrong based on your own or someone else's identities. This could be in college, in high school, in your family or neighborhood, at work, or in community service. In as much detail as possible, write about what happened. (6 minutes)

b. In as much detail as possible, write about how that made you feel. (4 minutes)

c. In as much detail as possible, write about what actions you took. (4 minutes)

3. *Journal Debrief* (5 minutes). Invite a few comments about the experience of conjuring a memory and of writing about it. Encourage participants to keep this in mind as they create their leadership action plan for an issue they care about. Possible debrief questions:

a. What was the journaling process like for you?

b. How might journaling help with understanding situations, actions, and what is needed for change?

4. *Leadership Action Plan* (50 minutes).

a. Individual Reflection (30 minutes). Distribute the action plan handout and have participants begin reflecting on the first page. Encourage the participants to think back to their journal primer and reflect on an issue they care about. Building from the first sheet, they then begin to consider actions and accountability for completing them. Encourage participants to use the handout to help them be as specific as possible as to how they can move forward with their desired actions.

b. Sharing and Discussion (20 minutes). Depending on the group size, bring the group into one circle, smaller circles, or pairs and share an action step from their plan. Brainstorm ideas and commitments for accountability and allyship needs from the group. Seek connections to leadership development and how these actions can relate to other issues or strategies for change. Consider the questions:

i. How can our group support you in your action plan?

ii. How does your action plan reflect your understanding of leadership?

5. *Wrap-Up and Gratitude* (3 minutes).

Facilitator Notes

- During the journal primer, use this prompt: "Pen to paper, respond to the following prompt." When time is up, prompt them to put their writing utensils down, and then present the next prompt and instruct them to pick up their writing utensils and proceed.

- Familiarize yourself with the prompts and the Leadership Action Plan worksheet. It might be useful to encourage the participants to utilize each other if they are stuck on a specific section of the worksheet.

- Be prepared to offer examples to assist participants in their reflections; consider a personal unjust situation and how that might connect to a specific social justice issue.

- Keep in mind that action is not always energy depleting, but can and should be energy inducing. For example, self-care, self-love, and self-respect or creating spaces for healing are all actions that can add sustaining energy.

References

Harro, B. (2000). The cycle of liberation. In M. Adams, W. J. Blumenfeld, R. Castañeda, H. W. Hackman, M. L. Peters, & X. Zúñiga (Eds.), *Readings for diversity and social justice* (pp. 618–625). Routledge.

Love, B. J. (2013). Developing a liberatory consciousness. In M. Adams, W. J. Blumenfeld, R. Castañeda, H. W. Hackman, M. L. Peters, & X. Zúñiga (Eds.), *Readings for diversity and social justice* (3rd ed.). (pp. 601–605). Routledge.

Biographies

Maritza Torres, PhD, is the assistant director for the LEAD Scholars Academy at the University of Central Florida. She researches Latinx leadership and culturally relevant leadership learning.

Erica Wiborg is a PhD candidate in the higher education program at Florida State University, where she works in the Leadership Learning Research Center as a research assistant; her research focuses on critical race theory, critical pedagogy, and Whiteness in leadership education and scholarship.

Handout 8.3.1: Leadership Action Plan

Awareness: What needs to change for both me and the system?	
Individual	**Systemic**
Beliefs	**Rules & Procedures**
Socialization	**Assumptions**

Awareness: What needs to change for both me and the system?	
Individual	**Systemic**
Knowledge	**Policies**

	Why does this change matter to you and your community?
Take a Pause	

Analysis: What can we do?

Brainstorm possible actions, such as educating, organizing, gaining inspiration, creating spaces for healing, transforming policies or cultures.

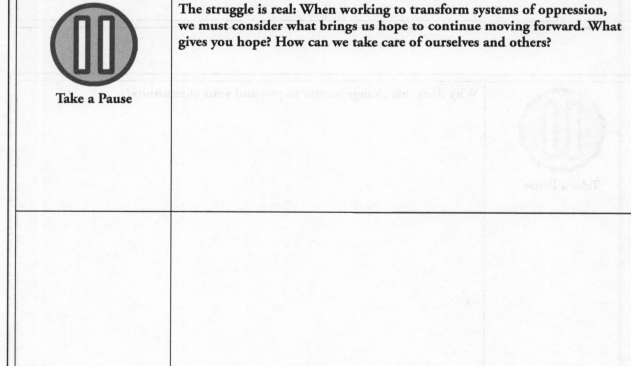

Take a Pause

The struggle is real: When working to transform systems of oppression, we must consider what brings us hope to continue moving forward. What gives you hope? How can we take care of ourselves and others?

Actions: What will you do?
Translate three of your potential actions from Analysis into action statements using a SMART format: specific, measurable, achievable, relevant, time-bound.
1.
2.
3.

Accountability & Allyship: Who and what do I need to support my change project?	
Resources What programs and services can you work with and learn from?	
People Who can support and challenge you?	
Agreements What do I need from others in order to be accountable for my actions and commitments (e.g., feedback, honesty, love)?	

Practicing Critical Hope in Leadership

Nolizwe M. Nondabula and Karin M. Cotterman

- Group size: 35 participants
- Time: 50 minutes
- Methods used: Self-reflection, group reflection, and group discussion
- Materials needed: Butcher paper, markers, Cycle of Liberation handout (created by the facilitator, using easily accessible images of Harro's work)

Overview

Harro's cycle of liberation (2007) is presented and participants are asked to consider their own paths of liberation while assessing cultural and structural influences of their leadership journey, including the oppressive systems and institutions we live and work within.

Learning Outcomes

- Understand and apply Harro's cycle of liberation
- Explore how cultural, institutional, and structural influences contributed to personal paths of liberation
- Practice intentionality of awareness and critical hope in the leadership journey

Directions

1. *Land Acknowledgment* (5 minutes). The facilitator will need to do some advance research and preparation to either create or identify an Indigenous Land Statement. Ideally, the Indigenous Land Statement is informed by and with the blessings of indigenous student groups, faculty, and/or staff. You might also consider how land acknowledgement is something that happens in other settings on your campus.
2. *Review Community Agreements* (5 minutes). This assumes that the group has community agreements from previous sessions. If not, consider establishing some for this session.
3. *Short Large Group Conversation* (5 minutes). "Given the multitude of intersectional lived experiences, what does womxn's liberation look, feel, sound, and smell like?"
4. *Review Harro's Cycle of Liberation* (10 minutes). Ask students if they've heard of Harro's cycle of liberation. While reviewing the cycle, the facilitator can model it with a personal journey, focusing on gender and leadership. After modeling, ask students if they have any questions and/or need any clarification on different stages of the cycle.

5. *Individual Reflection* (5 minutes). Distribute Cycle of Liberation handout to all students. Provide students time to individually reflect on the cycle, in writing, based on guiding questions provided on butcher paper.
   a. At what stage do you see yourself in this cycle?
   b. How did you get to your current stage?
   c. What's an experience that signifies your current or former stage?

6. *Small Group Conversation* (10 minutes). Ask students to break into four groups and reflect as a group on specific areas of the cycle of liberation:
   a. Group 1: Focus on Waking Up
   b. Group 2: Focus on Getting Ready and Reaching Out
   c. Group 3: Focus on Building Community and Coalescing
   d. Group 4: Focus on Creating Change and Maintaining

7. *Large Group Debrief* (10 minutes). Recap the activity by reflecting the shared language of students' experiences, acknowledge the uncommon or unique experiences shared, and close by offering appreciation in bringing themselves into the activity. The following questions might assist:
   a. What did you discuss as a group and notice from this exercise?
   b. What did you realize about yourself during this activity?
   c. What was difficult or uncomfortable in hindsight?
   d. Are there any limitations and/or critiques to this cycle?
   e. At the core of this cycle is self-love, joy, and support. Where do you find these core elements in your work and life?
   f. As you're developing yourself as an advocate for social change within these oppressive systems, how do you remain hopeful?
   g. What skills will you continue to build upon to get to liberation?
   h. What does it mean to liberate our practice of leadership?

Facilitator Notes

- In preparation for the session, the facilitator should draw the cycle of liberation on butcher paper/whiteboard or project it for students to see while modeling a personal journey. Also, post the personal reflection questions for students to see and refer back to during their personal reflection.
- Be prepared to define some terms such as "womxn" and create space for multiple definitions and interpretations of gender identity. Depending on where students are in their personal journey, it might be helpful to have certain definitions ready, such as intersectionality, gender identity, nonbinary, coalescing, collusion, womxn, ethnicity and race, and so on.
- Anticipate explaining and talking about Harro's cycle of socialization and how it connects to the cycle of liberation.
- Some important notes about the cycle of liberation and our experience of it:
  - The cycle of liberation isn't always linear (i.e., the waking up moment is not always a singular big incident . . . it can be the buildup of many incidents).
  - How do we leave space for mistakes, humility, and personal development in our leadership journey?
  - How do students exercise cultural humility while defining liberation for themselves while being mindful that liberation may look different for a peer?
- The authors would like to acknowledge Fernando Enciso-Marquez, who created an earlier version of this exercise that has since been adapted.

Reference

Harro, B. (2007). Cycle of socialization. In Adams, M., Bell, L. A., & Griffin, P. *Teaching for diversity and social justice*. Routledge.

Biographies

Nolizwe M. Nondabula (they/them) is a queer U.S.-born South African social justice educator and practitioner and the executive director of CommunityGrows, which cultivates healthy youth through growing gardens in low-income, diverse communities in San Francisco.

Karin M. Cotterman has worked in campus–community partnerships for over 20 years, and her research interests include race and place-based work and anti-racist White identity development. She is director of Engage San Francisco, at the University of San Francisco.

Diverse Levers for Social Change and Personal Action

Kristen Wright

- Group size: Open to any size group
- Time: 70 minutes
- Methods: Presentation, group discussion, group activity, reflection
- Materials: "Forms of Civic Engagement" handout, printout of statements for continuum activity, paper for individual reflection and group activity
- Variations: For groups larger than 25, split into smaller sets

---

Overview

The purpose of this activity is to introduce participants to the idea that there are diverse levers for social change and also to explore the ways in which social and cultural learning can inform the way we engage in civic engagement behaviors. Participants will examine their own understanding and experience with civic engagement, learn about the way others view civic engagement, and apply their learning to real community change. The guiding document for this activity is the forms of civic engagement list (Owen & Wagner, 2012).

Learning Outcomes

- Understand the different forms of civic engagement (Owen & Wagner, 2010)
- Critically reflect on individual experiences with social change behaviors and the impact of social and cultural forces on these experiences
- Apply understanding of levers for social change to addressing real life community concerns

Directions

1. *Introduction* (5 minutes). Introduce the idea that there are several ways for individuals and groups to engage with civic engagement and social change, and provide participants with a few examples of civic engagement behaviors:
   a. Investing a Saturday morning cleaning up a neighborhood park
   b. Donating $50 to a local nonprofit organization
   c. Facilitating a voter education program
   d. Serving as an Americorps VISTA Member
2. *Reflection & Sharing* (10 minutes). Ask participants to reflect on their own engagement with social change, offering the

following guiding questions. Then, provide two or three participants the opportunity to share their reflections with the larger group.

a. How do you define civic engagement?

b. In what ways have you engaged in civic engagement over the last year?

c. Why did you decide to participate in these particular activities?

d. Were there specific leaders who influenced your participation?

3. *Define Civic Engagement* (2 minutes). Explain that there are different definitions of civic engagement, but that one definition offered by the Pew Partnership for Civic Change is: "The will and capacity to solve public problems" (Owen & Wagner, 2010).

4. *Continuum Experience* (15 minutes). Using this definition and their own experience with civic engagement, invite participants to stand if they are able and arrange themselves along a continuum with one side of the room representing "highly likely" and the other side of the room representing "highly unlikely." Share that you will read a series of five statements describing a civic engagement behavior. Ask participants to arrange themselves along the continuum based on how likely they are to engage with social change in that way. Inform participants that after reading each statement you would like them to discuss their reason for selecting that place on the continuum with one or two individuals standing in the same area. Encourage participants to pay attention to similarities in identity, background, experience, and so forth. Before reading the statements, remind participants that there is no right or wrong answer and ask everyone to be honest with themselves as they select a place on the continuum. Example statements:

a. Write a letter to your Congressional representative asking them to vote in favor of specific legislation

b. Tutoring youth in an after-school program

c. Running for a political position in local government

d. Boycotting the purchase of products from a specific company because of unjust labor practices

e. Conducting research with a local community-based organization on the prevalence of lead paint in low-income housing units

5. *Brief Information Sharing* (5 minutes). After the continuum exercise, share the list of forms of individual civic engagement (Owen & Wagner, 2010) and provide participants time to read through the entire list, noting the form of engagement associated with the behaviors in which they are most likely to engage.

a. direct service

b. community research

c. education and advocacy

d. social innovation

e. political involvement

f. socially responsible personal and professional behavior

g. philanthropic giving

h. participation in associations

6. *Large Group Conversation* (10 minutes). Once participants have had time to read through the list, ask them to share some of their observations from the activity and the full list using guided questions.

a. What are your initial reactions and observations based on the activity?

b. While doing this activity, did any assumptions about what forms of civic engagement are "best" surface for you or members of your group? If so, what kind of assumptions and why do you think you held those beliefs?

c. How might power or privilege relate to the forms of civic engagement?

d. How do you think identities like gender, socioeconomic status, race, and so on impact the way individuals and groups engage with civic engagement?

7. *Small Group Discussion* (10 mins). After allowing for discussion on the large group activity, transition to the final activity by reminding participants that no single form of civic engagement or lever for social change is the right way to impact change, but by understanding collaboration and the influence of power and social structures on change efforts, individuals and groups can maximize change efforts. Break participants into groups

of three or four (depending on size). Once in their groups, ask participants to consider a local issue or challenge facing their community. Using the Forms of Civic Engagement list, invite participants to discuss the role of each form of civic engagement and how it contributes to addressing that local challenge. Instruct participants to consider power dynamics and the role of institutions (nonprofits and government) while they complete the activity.

8. *Debrief* (10 mins). Using the questions outlined as follows, or other questions specific to the participants, facilitate a conversation that addresses all components of the activity and participants' understanding of diverse levers for social change.

   a. What did you notice about the forms of civic engagement during this activity?

   b. How do power dynamics influence each of the forms of civic engagement?

   c. Do any of the forms of civic engagement require social or political capital to be most effective?

   d. How do you see yourself engaging with this issue? What form(s) of engagement do you feel most drawn to?

   e. What new learning or insights emerged for you today?

Facilitator Notes

It is important to acknowledge with participants that all forms of civic engagement have their role in creating positive social change in society, *and* to go a step deeper and critically review the influence of systems and power on the way individuals seek to create change in their communities. It is likely, and important, that these conversations bring up dialogue around identity and privilege. If participants have limited experience discussing power, privilege, or identity, it is important to add an explanation of terms or to provide additional reflection questions specific to your group and the way these concepts interact with civic engagement. Exploring the benefits of all forms of civic engagement, as well as the way they interact with one another, can help break

down barriers to participation and examine stereotypes about various forms of civic engagement.

Optional Homework for Further Reflection

As a homework assignment, you might direct students to the website for the Stanford University Haas Center for Public Service and its Pathways of Public Service and Civic Engagement project (https://haas.stanford.edu/about/about-our-work/pathways-public-service). The project defines six Pathways of Public Service:

- Community Engaged Learning and Research: Connecting coursework and academic research to community-identified concerns to enrich knowledge and inform action on social issues.
- Community Organizing and Activism: Involving, educating, and mobilizing individual or collective action to influence or persuade others.
- Direct Service: Working to address the immediate needs of individuals or a community, often involving contact with the people or places being served.
- Philanthropy: Donating or using private funds or charitable contributions from individuals or institutions to contribute to the public good.
- Policy and Governance: Participating in political processes, policymaking, and public governance.
- Social Entrepreneurship and Corporate Social Responsibility: Using ethical business or private sector approaches to create or expand market-oriented responses to social or environmental problems.

As part of the Pathways project, the Haas Center for Public Service has developed a free diagnostic tool to help students explore how their interests and skills can help contribute to the common good (https://stanforduniversity.qualtrics.com/jfe/form/SV_b8cK-NfgCHRI9TSt). You can instruct students to take the self-assessment and write a reflection about how this assessment creates insights and/or invites questions about themselves; you can ask students to explore what it looks like to exercise leadership in each of these pathways.

Reference	Biography
Owen, J. E., & Wagner, W. (2010). Situating service-learning in the context of civic engagement. In B. Jacoby & P. Mutascio (Eds.), *Looking in, reaching out: A reflective guide for community service-learning professionals* (pp. 231–253). Campus Compact.	**Kristen Wright** is the director of civic engagement through the Office of Undergraduate Education at George Mason University; she also chairs the board of directors for the IMPACT Conference.

Two-Minute Speeches Inspired by "Ain't I a Woman?"

Arnèle Francis and Rukan Said

- Group size: any
- Estimated time: 40 minutes
- Materials: paper, pens, copies of "Ain't I a Woman?" by Sojourner Truth
- Multimedia: You may choose to show video clips of the performance of Truth's speech (available at https://www.theso journertruthproject.com/the-readings).

Overview

Guided by the speech "Ain't I a Woman?" by Sojourner Truth, students will explore the question, "What are your purpose, person, and process of leadership?"

Learning Outcomes

- Explore collectively what Sojourner Truth tells us about today
- Articulate their purpose, person, and process of leadership
- Gain confidence in public speaking and public claiming of their leadership

Directions

1. *Quiet Reading* (5 minutes). Participants will read "Ain't I a Woman?" quietly. You may also choose to show a reading of the speech. Ask students to write down initial responses and questions evoked by the speech.
2. *Group Conversation* (10 minutes). The facilitator will open up a conversation about reactions, questions, and connections between the reading and leadership, connecting to questions of intersectionality, purpose, power, and the process of leadership.
3. *Prep: Two-Minute Speeches* (10 minutes). Using the speech as a reference, students will then generate their own two-minute speeches. They can write them down verbatim or create talking points. What is their purpose, person, and process of leadership?
4. *Sharing Out & Debrief* (15 minutes). Depending on the size of the group, invite students to share their two-minute speeches to the entire group or in smaller groups.

Facilitator Notes

The aim of this activity is for students to be reminded that the multiplicity and intersectionality of their own identities asserts that their voices are their own. While learning about concepts such as identity and intersectionality can be rather overwhelming, it invites students to see themselves fully and to understand how power is at play internally and in the systems of the world.

For a current take on intersectionality and women's leadership, consider sharing with students this interview of Stacey Abrams at the Chicago Humanities Festival (available at https://www.youtube.com/watch?v=F0e-ra5IrcA) where she discusses her book *Lead From the Outside: How to Build Your Future and Make Real Change* (2019). Ask yourself and students: How is Stacey Abrams and her political leadership an answer to Sojourner Truth's question?

References

Abrams, S. (2019). *Lead from the outside: How to build your future and make real change*. Picador.

Biography

Arnèle Francis is a proud Black woman from the twin-island federation of St. Kitts and Nevis; she has a BA in Integrative Studies with a concentration in Legal Studies, and minors in Women and Gender Studies and Social Justice from George Mason University and plans to pursue law.

Rukan Said is a Black feminist scholar, facilitator, writer, and speaker.

Index

The Coach's Guide for Women Professors

Who Want a Successful Career and a Well-Balanced Life

Rena Seltzer

Foreword by Frances Rosenbluth

"This book has something for *all* women in academia. Traditionally, the academy has been governed by unwritten rules that determine academic career success. Through the lived experiences of women faculty, *The Coach's Guide for Women Professors* sheds light on those unwritten rules in order to help women navigate successfully around them. This book offers just the right tools."—**Gloria D. Thomas,** *Director, Center for the Education of Women, University of Michigan*

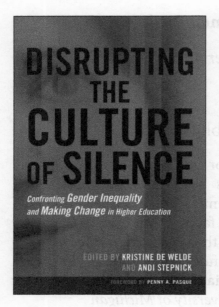

Disrupting the Culture of Silence

Confronting Gender Inequality and Making Change in Higher Education

Edited by Kristine De Welde and Andi Stepnick

Foreword by Penny A. Pasque

"Engagingly written and rich in formal data and telling anecdote, this sociologically smart collection will be an important tool for graduate students and faculty confronting what remains a male-biased system of higher education. The editors draw on their own interviews with women in many academic disciplines and enlist other researchers and activists to provide a rich and deep look at gendered experiences in academia today. Commendably, the editors give strong representation to women of color, disabled women, and lesbians in defining how 'women' experience (and overcome) diverse challenges. Variation among disciplines and between institutions is also highlighted. The beauty of the volume emerges most in its telling details: for example, the problematic idea that 'just say no' to service work is a feasible organizational strategy; the value in changing policy rather than seeking ad hoc accommodations; the self-contradictory advice about when in an academic career to have a baby. An excellent bibliography and list of disciplinary and other extra-university resources for change make this book an invaluable resource for all faculty or students looking for insight into strategies for real inclusivity. Summing up: Highly recommended. Upper-division undergraduates and above."—**Choice**, *reviewed by Myra Marx Ferree, University of Wisconsin*

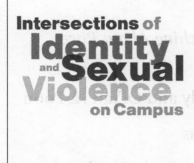

Intersections of Identity and Sexual Violence on Campus

Centering Minoritized Students' Experiences

Edited by Jessica C. Harris and Chris Linder

Foreword by Wagatwe Wanjuki

From the Foreword:

"I am amazed and humbled by the opportunity to introduce the contents of this book. It may sound like hyperbole when I say, 'It changed my life,' but I honestly cannot think of a better way to describe its impact on my beliefs on organizing to eradicate sexual violence—on campuses and off. *Intersections* outlines what I've needed as a survivor during my times as a student and activist; this book should be mandatory reading for every individual who works with the issue of campus gender-based violence. Journalists, activists, and administrators alike stand to gain the knowledge needed to spur the transformative work of a power-conscious, history-informed, and intersectional understanding of the dynamics of sexual violence."—**Wagatwe Wanjuki,** *Feminist Writer and Activist*

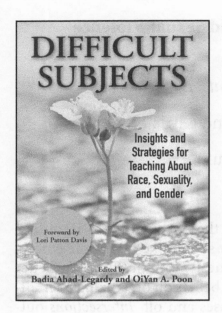

Difficult Subjects

Insights and Strategies for Teaching About Race, Sexuality, and Gender

Edited by Badia Ahad-Legardy and OiYan A. Poon

Foreword by Lori Patton Davis

"Both teaching and learning are deeply social endeavors, shaped by our identities, involving interactions across multiple axes of difference, and often taking place within high-stakes contexts. This volume is a crucial intervention not only in illuminating the many challenges we face as university faculty who want to teach 'difficult subjects' but in providing a road map for many who themselves have been cast as 'difficult subjects' to find ways to be effective and to thrive in the academy. Extremely timely, this book provides both new and veteran critical educators with critical insights for doing our work in these tough times. Together, the experiences and the concrete strategies shared across the chapters of this volume help provide a roadmap for navigating changing university environments and for persisting in the crucial work of teaching students to think critically about race, gender and sexuality. This book is a must-read for both those who are new to the classroom and those who are looking for support and sustenance to persist."—**Amanda E. Lewis,** *Professor of African-American Studies and Sociology, and Director of the Institute for Research on Race and Public Policy, University of Illinois at Chicago*

Digital Leadership in Higher Education

Purposeful Social Media in a Connected World

Josie Ahlquist

"Effective leadership means we must bring our values and mission—not just soundbites—to our activity in the digital sphere. And it's not as hard as you may think, thanks to the very practical examples and exercises Josie Ahlquist has given us in this book."**—Brandon Busteed,** *President, University Partners, Kaplan, Inc.*

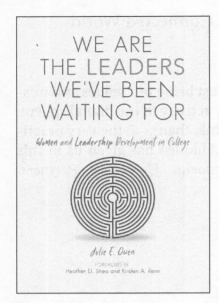